WALKING
– with Wanderer –

Exploring the Hills around Langholm

Walking With Wanderer

Published by The Langholm Initiative, 98 High Street, Langholm, Dumfriesshire DG13 0DH, December 2000.

© Alex Carruthers 2000
Photographs by Alex Carruthers, Roger Smith and Mike Tinker

All rights reserved. No part of this publication may be reproduced, stored in a retrieval system, or transmitted, in any form or by any means, electronic, mechanical, photocopying, recording or otherwise, without the prior permission of The Langholm Initiative.

Front cover: Warbla from Castle Hill above Langholm
Photo by Mike Turner.   Cover design by Tony Key

ISBN 0-9539767-0-X

£6.95

CONTENTS

Introduction		5
Glossary		9
Local Place Names		10
1:	Perambulating the Muckle Toon	15
2:	A Langholm Hills Circuit	20
3:	The Tarras Aqueduct	23
4:	Jenny Noble's Gill	26
5:	Out to Crumpton	28
6:	Jock's Hope and the Lady Florance Stone	31
7:	Warbla	34
8:	Pike Fell and Unthank Pikes	36
9:	Ettrick Pen	39
10:	Target Burn and Whita Hill	41
11:	Potholm and Castle Hills	43
12:	Arkleton Craigs	45
13:	The Becks	47
14:	Calkin and Boykenhopehead	49
15:	The Craig Burn	51
16:	Tarras Lodge to Perterburn	53
17:	The Langfauld and Potholm	55
18:	Mosspeeble and Bloody Gill	56
19:	Glencorf and Becks	58
20:	Glenrief	61
21:	Penton Linns	63
22:	Tansy Hill and Arresgill	65
23:	Hartsgarth and Roan Fell	67
24:	Peden's View	69
25:	Tarras Water and Whita	72
26:	Tinnis Hill and the Horned Cairn	74
27:	Langholm to Meikledale	76
28:	Meikledale to Langholm	78

INTRODUCTION

This book brings together a collection of articles describing just some of the many walks I have taken over the years in the hills and glens of Eskdale and the surrounding area, from my home in Langholm. It is not intended as a detailed guidebook. These are personal reminiscences, and as some of the walks were taken a number of years ago, things on the ground may have changed. The countryside is a surprisingly dynamic place!

I hope that the book will however provide an insight into the landscape, culture and history of this beautiful area and will transmit some of the pleasure I have gained from exploring it over so many years. Detailed maps are not provided, but inquisitive and experienced walkers should be able to pick up the line of many of the walks, using OS Landranger sheet 79.

Some general advice on walking in the countryside may be useful.

Dogs must be kept on leads in fields containing sheep and lambs and under close control in fields containing cows as well as at all other times. One word of warning, cows can be extremely protective and as a result, more dangerous than bulls in the protection of a new born calf. If you must pass through a field containing cows with new born calves or where a cow is calving - give them a wide berth. If you are accompanied by a dog, keep it off the lead but strictly to heel. If a cow should approach out of curiosity it is safer to send your dog away than to have an irate mother near you!

Under Scottish Rights of Way legislation a bull may be pastured in a field with a public footpath passing through as long as the bull is being run with cows or heifers.

Gateway to the hills

INTRODUCTION

Great care should be taken during the lambing season from early March to late May, during calving in April/May, during grouse shooting on the hills and muirs from the twelfth of August through to December, and during pheasant shooting in the woods from November to the end of January.

The Act of Trespass in Scotland does exist, but an offence is not committed in Scottish Law simply by being there; damage must be proved and a court order taken out. Conversely, Rights of Way must run from one public place to another and must have been used for at least twenty years. On the whole the Scottish system works, probably because mutual tolerance, goodwill, commonsense and courtesy can often be more effective than the might and majesty of the law!

On longer walks or during inclement weather your equipment should include boots, waterproofs, spare sweater, survival bag and a hat. Jeans are not recommended as once they become wet they remain wet and cold. A serious walker always carries; map 79 and a compass, a whistle (a series of six blasts should summon help) and some energy sweets such as glucose or Kendal Mint Cake; just in case!

The Langholm Walks Project

During 1999 and 2000, the public agencies in the area, working through the Langholm Initiative, put considerable effort into developing a network of waymarked walks routes. The result was the Langholm Walks Project, which led in August 2000 to the launch by Magnus Magnusson KBE, in his capacity as Chairman of the Paths For All Partnership, of an initial network of ten walks. Most of these walks are based upon routes included in this book and first described in my regular articles in the *Eskdale & Liddesdale Advertiser*, and I am delighted to have played a part in this splendid initiative, which will provide visitors with a safe and welcoming introduction to the delight of walking my 'hills of home'.

A booklet describing the ten walks is available locally price 50p, or by post from The Langholm Initiative, 98 High Street, Langholm, Dumfriesshire DG13 0DH. You can even visit a website at: www.langholmwalks.co.uk. How things have changed!

The first chapter of the book describes a walk around Langholm itself, to introduce readers to the character of the 'Muckle Toon' from where so many of the walks described start. A Town Trail leaflet, giving more detail on many of the historic and interesting buildings and places in Langholm, is also available from the address above, price 50p.

INTRODUCTION

Acknowledgements

Many of the articles in this book are based upon material supplied for my regular articles in the *Eskdale & Liddesdale Advertiser*, and I am grateful to them for the opportunities they have provided me over the years, and for permission to reproduce the material here. The Wanderer thanks his two companions on these walks and on innumerable others; Tara my yellow labrador and Corrie my black labrador, and would acknowledge the invaluable information gleaned from the late Sir Edward Johnson-Ferguson's *Place Names of Dumfriesshire*.

Finally always follow the Country Code;
1. Keep dogs under control as above.
2. Protect wildlife.
3. Guard against fire.
4. Use stiles or gates and leave them as you find them.
5. Do not obstruct entrances or gateways.
6. Keep to paths across farmland or crops.
7. Do not interfere with livestock or machines
8. Take your litter home with you.
9. Have a wee blether with anyone you meet. You might just learn something!

GLOSSARY

I recently met some visitors who did not understand some words used during my peregrinations, so I have listed the more common ones, remembering that Scots was a language rather than a dialect of English with words derived from Gaelic, Norse, Old English and French as well as its own indigenous words.

Allt, Burn	-	Stream
Auld, Sean	-	Old
Bairn, Wean	-	Child
Ban, Bhan	-	White
Bar	-	Summit or top
Bauchle	-	Down at heel person
Buachaille	-	Shepherd or herdsman
Bealach	-	Pass or saddle
Beg or Beag	-	Small, little
Ben, Pen	-	Mountain or Hill
Bield	-	Shelter
Biggin	-	Building
Brig	-	Bridge
Bucht, Stell, Fauld	-	Sheep pen
Clamjamphrey	-	Odds and ends
Carse, Holm	-	River meadow
Cleuch, Heuch, Gill	-	Gully, ravine
Craig	-	Crag, cliff
Cundy	-	Small covered watercourse
Dauner or Dander	-	Stroll
Dearg	-	Red
Dod, Knock, Knowe	-	Rounded Hill
Druim or Drum	-	Ridge
Dubh, Dou	-	Black or Dark
Drookit	-	Absolutely soaked
Drystane Dyke	-	Wall of dry stones
Fettle	-	Condition or fitness
Fion, Fiona	-	Fair, Fair One
Forfaughtan	-	Worn out
Garbh (garve)	-	Rough
Gowan	-	Daisy
Glaur	-	Mud, the sticky variety
Gowk	-	Cuckoo
Grain	-	Confluence of burns
Horny Gollach, Gellock	-	Earwig

Howe	-	Hollow
Lane, Pol	-	Slow stream
Larach	-	Ancient foundation
Laverock	-	Lark
Machair	-	Level grassy shoreland
Meall, Mill	-	Hill
Meikle	-	Much
Muckle	-	Big, Large
Mirk	-	Gloaming, Twilight
More or Mhor	-	Great, big
Muir	-	Moorland
Neuk, Cuil, Wrae	-	A Corner
Og	-	Young
Pech	-	Pant, Gasp
Reiver	-	Robber or Raider (Borders)
Sauch	-	Willow
Scaur	-	Scar, Cliff
Scunnered	-	Disgusted, sickened
Shank	-	Sloping ridge, buttress
Shaw, ska	-	Small wood
Sheiling	-	Shepherd's summer dwelling
Smeddum	-	Pith, Vigour
Snell	-	Bitter cold
Snod	-	Trim, neat, tidy
Spiel	-	Climb
Stob	-	Pointed Hill
Strushel	-	Disorderly, untidy
Teallach	-	Hearth or forge
Teuchat	-	Peewit, Green plover
Todtails	-	Foxgloves
Toom, tuim	-	Empty
Traik, trauchle	-	Wearied trudge
Trod	-	Track or footpath
Whaup	-	Curlew

LOCAL PLACE NAMES

ABERLOSK	Bushy mouth of a river
AIRSWOOD	Erche (Irishman's) wood.
ALBIE RIG	Old farm on a ridge
ARCHERBECK	An orchard around a beck
AUCHENBEG	Small field
AUCHENDONNA	Bad or evil field
AUCHENRIVOCK	Brindled fields

BAILEY HILL	Village or signal fire
BARNGLIESH	Hill of the church
BARNTALLOCH	Hill of the forges
BARRASCROFTS	A tilt yard on a croft
BIRRENS	Heap of stones, burial place.
BLOCH (Bealach)	A pass
BOGRIE	A boggy place
BOMBIE	Free landholder
BURNGRAINS	Confluence of streams
BRUNTSHIELBOG	A burnt? shieling in a bog
BUACHAILLE (Bauchle) HILL	Herdsman's hill
CAMRA (Kemra)	A curved fort
CANONBIE	The farm of the Canon
CAREWOODRIG	Fort on ridge or Rocky ridge
CARLINTOOTH	Witch's tooth
CARRUTHERS	Caer Ridderch, Ridderch's fort
CASSOCK	A steep ascent
COPSHAWHOLM	A wooded knowe in a river meadow
CRONKSBANK	Bank of the crane or heron?
CROOKHOLM	A meadow at a bend in the river
CRUMPTON	A crooked enclosure or the town of Crump
CUIL	A corner
DORNEY GILL	Pebbly gill
DOUGLEN	The black glen
DOWNEY HILL	Hill of the fortress
DRUMLANRIG	Clearing on a wooded ridge
DUMLINNS	Fort by a linn
EAGLESFIELD	Field of the Church
ENZIEHOLM	A meadow in a nook
EWES	Water
EWESLEES	Forest clearing by the river
FINGLAND (Fion glen)	Fair glen
FLOSH	A marshy place
GABER GILL (gabhar)	Ravine of the goats
GARWALD (garbh allt)	Rough stream
GILNOCKIE	Small hill by a ravine
GLEDSNEST	Kite's Nest
GLENBEAG	Small glen
GLENCARTHOLM	A holm near a glen with a fast stream
GLENCORF	Glen of the memorial
GLENDEARG	Red glen
GLENDIVAN	Deep glen
GLENDOW	Black glen
GLEN EROCH	Easterly glen?
GLENGAR	Rough glen

GLENMANNA	Monk's glen
GLEN MORE	Big glen
GLENSHANNA	Glen of the old ford
GLENVARREN	Glen of big rocks
GLENZIER	Short glen
GUILE HASS	Pass of the marigolds
HARTSGARTH	The enclosure of the stag
HOGHILL	Hill of the yearling sheep
HOWGILL	Hollow by the small glen
KNOTTY HOLM	Knotty - a game like shinty
LANGHOLM	Long meadow by the river
LOCKERBIE	Lockhart's farm
LOGAN HEID	A hollow (lagan) at the head of the glen
MEGGAT WATER	Boggy valley
MEIKLEDALE	Big valley
MOODLAW	A meeting hill
MUMBIEHIRST	Monkbiehirst - a monk's farm at a thick wood
NITTY HOLM	Small neat meadow
PINGLE	A struggle for survival
RAEGILL	Rae - roe deer
RASHIEL	Small summer dwelling in the rushes
RENNALD BURN	Scattered land held by a tenant
SHAW or SKA	Small wood
SHERRA CRAIGS	Sheriff's crags
SLACKHEAD	A Shallow wet valley
SORBIE HASS	Farm on a swampy pass
STAKEHEUCH	A secret place?
STAPLEGORDON	Pillar in a muddy ferm toon
STRUSHEL BURN	Disorderly or untidy stream
SWINGLE	Swine gill
TARCOON	A small rounded hill
TANLAWHILL	A beacon fire?
THICKSIDE	Thick - thatch
THORNIEWHATS	A clearing among thorn bushes
TIMPEN	A rounded hump
TOMSHIELBURN	Shepherd's summer hut by a hill stream
TOURNEY HOLM	Place of combat or jousts
TWIGLEES	Forest clearing
UNTHANK	A clearing occupied by squatters
WAULK MILL	A cloth mill
WARB or WARD LAW	Beacon Hill
WATCARRICK	Rocky ford
WAUCHOPE	Valley of the foreigners (Welsh)
WRAE HASS	A corner of good land on a pass

The beautiful Ewes Valley

Bonnie Langholm

"Bonnie Langholm! Flower of Eskdale!
Nestling neath old Whita's crest,
There, alone, mid Scotia's splendour
Lives the scene my heart loves best.
Stream and woodland, hill and valley,
Nature's choicest gifts are thine;
Like a wreath of glory round thee,
Gems of beauty rich entwine."

David J. Beattie

1. PERAMBULATING THE MUCKLE TOON

Some years ago, at the time of the Common Riding in July, I was asked to show a visitor around Langholm. On the appointed day he duly arrived; it was Jimmie Macgregor, researching and preparing a broadcast. The Muckle Toon is nowadays not very muckle at all, so an hour should have seen us round the houses. In the event it took us a lot longer!

We walked north along the High Street to the Townhead Church where we crossed the Langholm Bridge. In front of us lay Thomas Telford Road, named after the famous civil engineer who worked as a mason in Langholm and went on to design many bridges, canals and buildings all over Britain. Across the bridge we turned immediately right onto Frances Street and along the river to Mary Street, where we found the Masonic Lodge with its view across the Esk before we reached the Buccleuch Hall which has hosted many famous actors and singers. Beside us at the end of Montague Street stood the stone column of the Buccleuch Square Pump round which the Common Riding procession had earlier "perambulated"!

Our route took us between Langholm Academy and Langholm Primary School where Hugh MacDiarmid received his early education. At the end of Eskdaill Street we turned into Caroline Street and Buccleuch Terrace, and so along the bank of the Wauchope Water to the Park Bridge. In the Buccleuch Park we had a look at the award winning gardens, the War Memorial and the imposing Parish Church.

Back on Caroline Street we walked down to the Suspension Bridge over the River Esk. When it was officially opened in 1871, so many people rushed onto the structure that the puir thing

Langholm from the Kilngreen

collapsed in its middle. The story goes that during the rescue operations distraught parents would rush into the river, grab a child, look at it without recognition, exclaim "That's no' mine!" and throw the bairn back in again! Luckily the Esk was very low at the time.

Walking across the bridge we stopped to watch the antics of a variety of gulls and a couple of jenny herons while mallard ducks were feeding along the edge. Some of these ducks were decidedly odd, being black and brown with white splotches. Many years ago a zealous council official had transported a number of these mutations from Moffat where they had over-run the park. At first they had interbred with the local population, but now the genes of the genuine mallards appear to be winning. On the other end of the bridge we came to the Community Centre, the Day Centre and the Council Library, before going on up Charles Street to the Thomas Hope Hospital. It had originally been donated to the town by a benefactor and is now part of the local health board.

Sir Pulteney Malcolm

We passed through Wattie's Arch and back onto the busy High Street where the Town Hall, the Eskdale Hotel and the Post Office are all built from grey Whita sandstone. Behind the Town Hall we came to the Old Library Building which houses a small art gallery and the Langholm Library, used in his youth by MacDiarmid. Thomas Telford donated a sum of money to this library and to the Westerkirk Library; both libraries hold rare and valuable volumes. In the small garden in front is the ancient Mercat Cross and the 'Marble Man', a statue of Admiral Sir Pulteney Malcolm, one of Nelson's captains along with Admiral Hardy. Malcolm was Napoleon's warder on St Helena and was a 'son of the manse' from a family of 17 - four of whom were knighted.

We returned to the Market Place where next to the Eskdale Hotel, an old coaching inn, we went down the Laird's Entry. Here we found the remnants of some very small houses, most of which are now used for storage but where a century ago a dozen or so large families dwelt.

The Laird's Entry led us to Arthur Bell's Mill, to the Waverley Mill (Edinburgh Woollen Mills) and to the site of the former railway station and gasworks, now occupied by the Border Fine Arts factory and gallery. We were soon back onto the High Street where we turned left and crossed the road into a very attractive renovation where an old ruined mill and cottages had been converted into an area with small gardens and parking places. The lower part is still known as Parliament Square, where people formerly met to 'parley' or converse with one another, to pass on items of local and national news and of course gossip.

Two narrow lanes have been partly preserved, although the origin of the names is obscure; Joukers Close could mean a place where truants or double-dealers lived, while Wapping Lane could be derived from 'warping' or it could mean in Old Scots - common or vulgar. Once again we noted the size and number of the wee 'buts and bens' and realised how the town with less than half the present area could have had more than thrice the present population.

Next we turned up the steep Kirk Wynd where the horses and riders every Common Riding gallop at breakneck speed. Turning left into Drove Road, we made a diversion past the oldest occupied house in Langholm and turned right up Alma Place to the ruined kirk and old kirkyard. Immediately above the cemetery we could see Number 17 Arkinholm Terrace, where Hugh MacDiarmid had lived for much of his youth. Back on Drove Road we followed the Common Riding 'Route of the Heather Besoms' as it passed Arkinholm, once a millowner's mansion before becoming a nunnery for the Sisters of St. Francis. It is now again a private dwelling.

We dropped down to the main road and the Kilngreen. As the name implies, it was possibly the site of some lime kilns, but as there is neither workable coal nor lime in the immediate vicinity, could the name have arisen from the Battle of Arkinholm on this very site in 1455, when it might have been called Killing Green? This battle was one of the most important and far-reaching in Scottish history as the power of the Douglases was curtailed and the Stuart line was confirmed on the throne. Across the Esk we could see the ruins of Langholm Castle. Originally called Arkinholm, the town of Langholm was created a Burgh in 1621. We crossed the Ewes Bridge, north of the Kilngreen, to visit the Armstrong Trust Museum then returned to our starting place. It had taken us a lot longer than we had anticipated, having made frequent stops to look, to listen and to blether with folks.

You may have noticed during my discourse that many of the Langholm streets have been given Christian names. This is no coincidence; in the distant past as the town grew, each new street was given the name of a member of the families of the Dukes of Buccleuch and Queensberry.

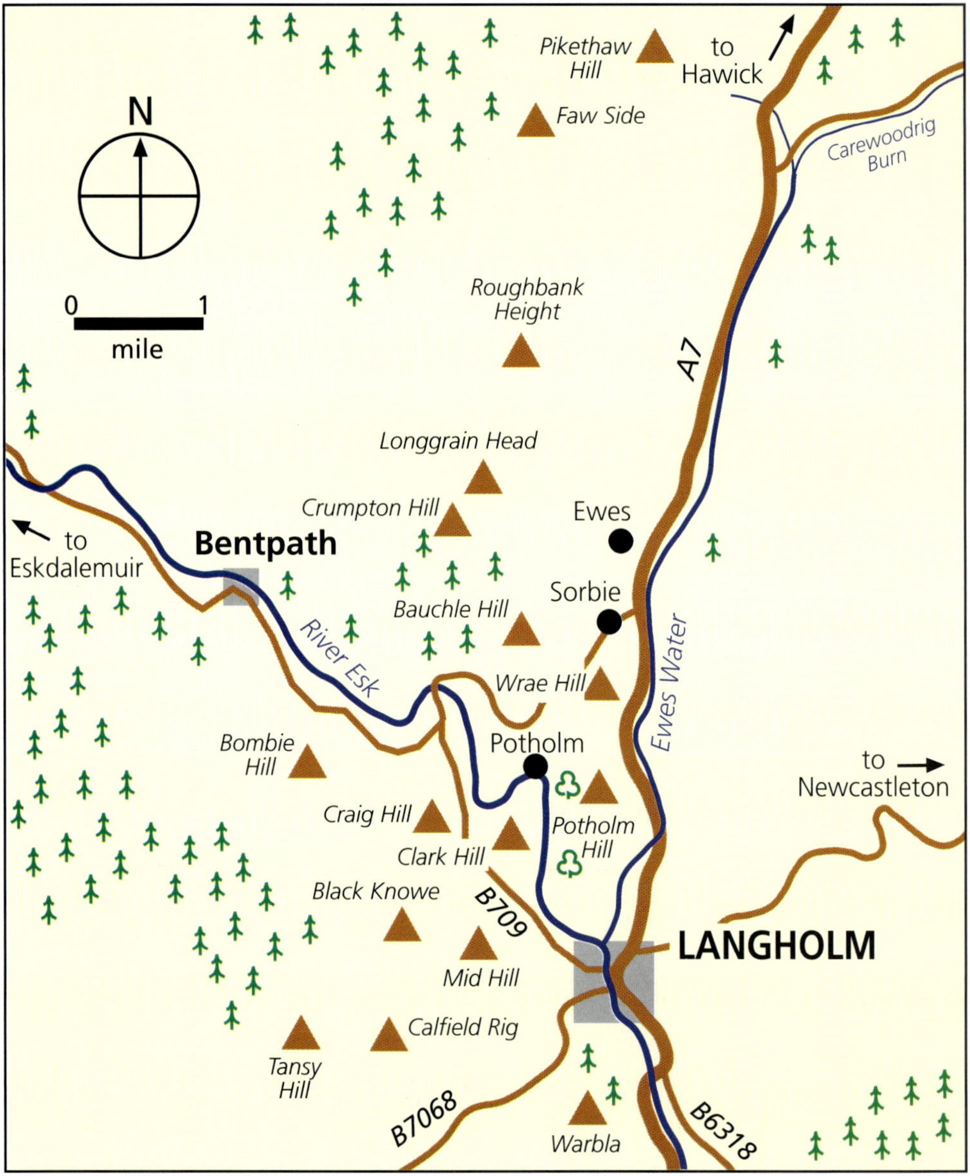
N
0
1
mile
Pikethaw Hill
to Hawick
Faw Side
Carewoodrig Burn
Roughbank Height
A7
Longgrain Head
Crumpton Hill
Ewes
to Eskdalemuir
Bentpath
Sorbie
Bauchle Hill
River Esk
Ewes Water
Wrae Hill
Bombie Hill
Potholm
to Newcastleton
Craig Hill
Potholm Hill
Clark Hill
Black Knowe
B709
LANGHOLM
Mid Hill
Calfield Rig
Tansy Hill
B7068
Warbla
B6318

WALKING WITH WANDERER

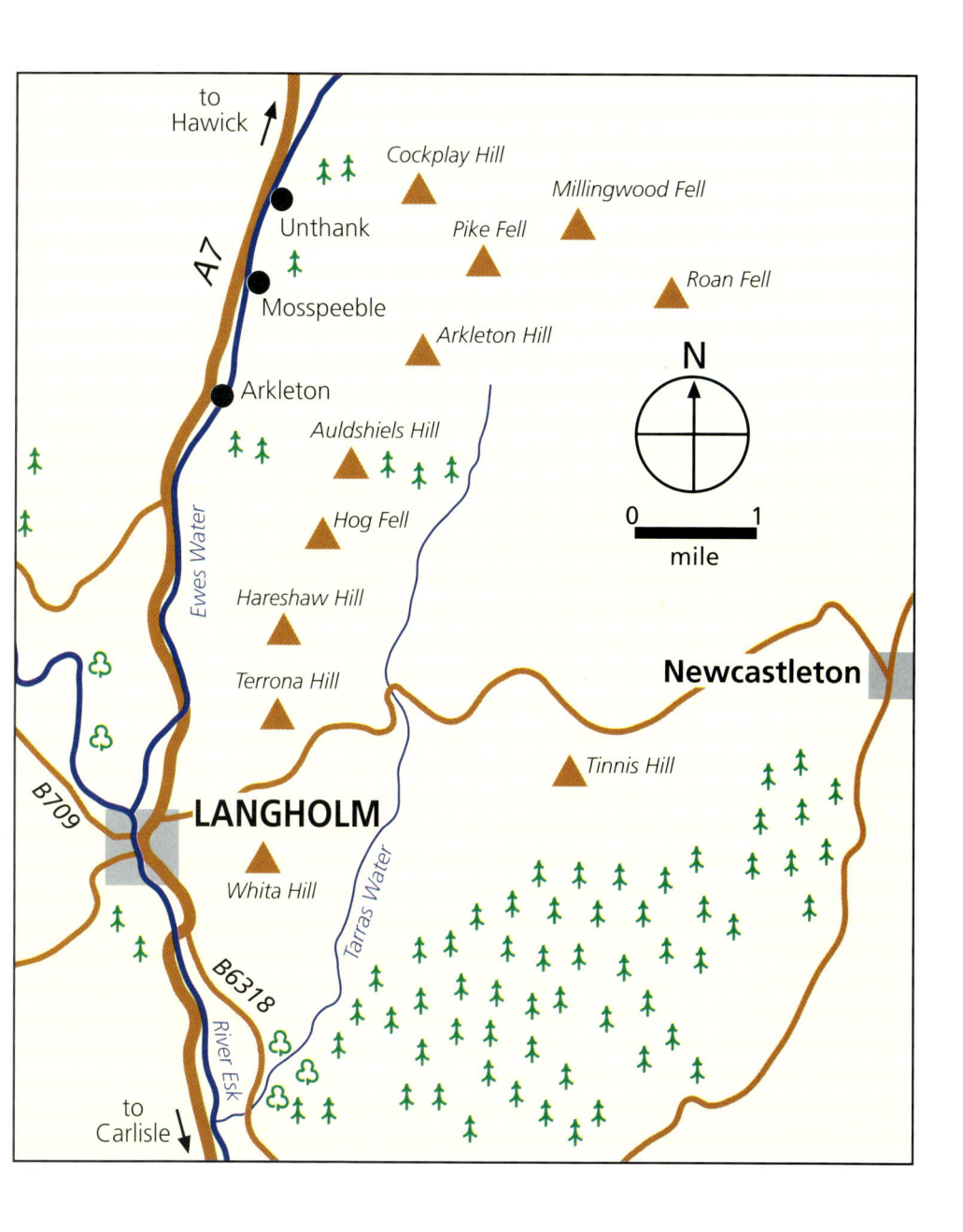

2: A LANGHOLM HILLS CIRCUIT

The weather was unsettled with prolonged showers and some sunshine, so we chose a walk that although around 11 miles in length, has numerous 'easy outs'. At no point is it more than three miles to Langholm. From that description you will have realised that the walk is roughly circular around the Muckle Toon hills.

We walked north from the Kilngreen and crossed the Ewes Bridge, following the road round to the right and uphill to Pathhead, then onwards to the next house before turning left on a rough track until the hill gate is reached. From there it was a steady grind to the top of the Castle Hill where, during April and May, I always take care that we do not disturb any calving Galloways that may be on the hill.

I kept looking back as the hills to the west and to the north gradually came into view; Criffel and Queensberry, Lowther Hill and Ettrick Pen. Soon, in spite of some rough walking, we reached the top and continued along until we reached a drystane dyke. As we were only a few hundred yards from the top of Potholm Hill we nipped along, admired the view and nipped back again to the dyke which we then followed downhill to the road, having completed our first hill - or was it the second?

Langholm from Whita Hill

Golf Hill and Bauchle Hill

Half a mile south on the A7 we reached the indicator for the MacDiarmid Memorial. We turned left and immediately left again onto a steep forestry road for half a mile until we reached an old cottage, now a byre, called Whiteshiels, but locally known as Whuchuls. From there we followed the edge of the wood until we crossed the Newcastleton road and, keeping the quarry on our right, we took to the hills once again. Whita had some very rough walking through the relics of the numerous small quarries which have now transformed themselves into overgrown points of interest and variety, rather than ecological desecrations.

And so to the top of Whita where 'The Monument' in honour of Sir John Malcolm was erected in 1835. Sir John was one of a family of 17 children of a minister from Burnfoot, Westerkirk. Four of the brothers became knighted from high government posts such as Governor General or Admiral. The views over the Lake District and the Solway are well worth the effort of getting here. On a very clear day I have even spied the Isle of Man.

From the Monument we followed the dyke due south as far as a corner gate where a bearing of 230 degrees took us to the 'Roon Hoose'. Just south of the Roon Hoose the well-worn track produced a branch to the right so we followed this until we reached a kissing gate leading onto the route of the former railway. After ascertaining that there were no trains, we turned right and walked as far as a gap in the left hand fence where a steep path took us down to the Skipper's Bridge. That was hill two, or was it three?

Two hundred yards over the bridge we turned up an unmade road which branches off uphill to the right. Just before the Skipper's Cottages we turned left through a gate and in ten yards turned right onto a faint track which we followed to the top of the slope. Nicholson's Knowe, the Kernigal Wood and Langholm lay below us and the way was clear across to Warbla. It is always a disappointment to me to reach the top of Warbla, festooned as it is with television relay masts. Such is progress! Here ended hill number three (or is it four).

From the west side of the mast we followed the old peat road downhill until we reached the first enclosed field where we dropped left in the direction indicated by the sign and so reached the wee gate right in the corner of the wood and only 50 yards from the Auld Stane Brig over the Wauchope Water.

Crossing the bridge we turned left up a tarmac road for three quarters of a mile and at the end of the wood, turned right into the Knowe Field; the ground at this wee gate can be gie glaury! We then followed the edge of the spruce wood until in 600 yards we crossed the Beck's Burn and went through a gate. Once again we followed a line of beech trees uphill as far as a corner gate from where we walked diagonally uphill to another gate and a sheep pen where we crossed to the Newlands Cleuch, locally known as the Peewit Burn.

Another 400 yards took us onto Meikleholm Hill which lay just through a gate in the March Dyke. It was only a quarter of a mile north-west to Mid Hill as shown on the map (OS79 345855) but locally known as Timpen. We went over Timpen and descended along the Green Sike to the road near the Craigcleuch quarry.

During lambing time I avoid the Knowe Field and the other fields around it by walking along the road into Langholm, turning left up a small lane beside the first of the houses and so to the top of Timpen. From the bottom of the Green Sike it was just a mile and a half past the Breconwrae and back into Langholm. And so we had completed the four hills - or should it be the six hills?

3: THE TARRAS AQUEDUCT

This is a fairly strenuous woodland walk of about 14 miles, which can be reduced to nine miles by parking near the top of Broomholm Hill, or even to seven miles by returning directly from Claygate. It is also a journey into our industrial past. Few visitors realise that there were two working coalfields in picturesque Eskdale from 1770 until the one at Archerbeck was abandoned in 1922. While they were in operation, a reserve supply of water was needed in time of drought to operate the pumping engines for the Byreburnfoot mine. The result was an aqueduct conveying water from the upper Tarras Valley to augment the Byre Burn. This of course meant crossing two deep cleuchs and forming a small reservoir at the head of the Lake Burn.

We took the car down the Penton road and at the top of Broomholm Hill, parked near the field gate on the right; very close to the remains of a Roman fort. We walked north-east up the side road past Broomholmshiels until in half a mile we could look across the Tarras 'beef tubs' where the Reivers used to hide stolen cattle. We could actually trace the route of the aqueduct as it ran in an irregular broken line alongside the spruce plantation, but we had still to reach the start of the water course near Cronksbank, a mile away.

The Tarras Water near Howgillcleuch

The Fairy Loup

Along the road, down the hill, over the bridge and back up again until just before Cronksbank the road crossed a man-made channel, half filled with sand and stones. The aqueduct had originated just up the valley but its channel was almost impassable due to a thick growth of bushes, briars and brambles, although we did eventually find a masonry retaining wall. Now that we were at the beginning of the aqueduct, we about-turned to find the end. The old water channel appeared to be climbing ahead of us, but that was only an optical illusion; it had deteriorated in places to a muddy ditch with the feeder burns now cutting straight across. In some places the route was little more than a sheep trod while in other places there were traces of stone lining slabs.

At the Raegill, the aqueduct seemed to wander for about 200 yards up the deep gill before vanishing. Then on the other side I saw a short but high retaining wall. I slithered my way down the steep, wet, mossy banking and found that I was passing another such wall. I had found the piers of the long-gone wooden aqueduct! Once over the Raegill we followed the overgrown ditch below the spruce plantation until we reached a major obstacle; the even wider and steeper Howgillcleuch. But this time I knew what I was looking for among the hazels and willows and eventually found two opposing piers; we were still on track. I was told of an old man who had been paid to walk the length of the aqueduct every week to check for leaks or breaches. And all for one penny!

As we passed the small farm of Howgillcleuch the course of the aqueduct was easily picked out, but I was disconcerted when it divided into two with one branch running downhill to the Tarras. The remains of a sluice gate indicated that this must have been a flood release. The ground ahead seemed to rise! Probably over years of disuse, mosses and weeds had taken root and created a small raised bog. The route was clear into 'The

Lake' and hence to the Byreburn at Broomieknowe, where we joined the road to Byreburn Bridge, Claygate and Gilnockie Schoolhouse.

At this point we could have turned right and so back along the road to Langholm, but we went to the left, and at the bottom of the hill turned onto the road to the Fairy Loup (OS79 394783), an attractive wee waterfall situated in a sheltered glen abounding with early spring flowers and flamboyant wild summer blooms. We were only half a mile from the Esk and the old pump house.

At the river we were presented with some of the most attractive views of the Esk. Turning right we walked past the landslides which had closed the road to traffic. Immediately before Hollows (Gilnockie) Bridge we turned onto a rough road above the river. After a quick look at the larach of Gilnockie Castle on the left and for fossils in the rocky river bed we passed Shortsholm and kept straight on as far as the deep Hobb's Sike. Uphill along the sike, a faint path led us to a field where, keeping the fence on our right we encountered a disused Langholm railway cutting where we turned north along the railway track for a quarter of a mile (watching for trains) until we reached a well defined cross track, where we turned right.

Within the angle of these two tracks we had a look for the site of another rather large Roman camp which we should have been able to find, but it lies within a dense forest, although traces of the boundary earthworks can be seen. The camp is about 24 acres in extent and had probably been a temporary satellite of the camp at Netherby. When we eventually reached the Langholm road (B6318) we turned left and so made our way back to where we had started.

4: JENNY NOBLE'S GILL

This is an easy six-mile walk on road and tracks with the exception of one mile of rough walking along the west bank of the Tarras. Corrie and I walked from the Kilngreen, south to the Skipper's Bridge and kept straight on along the left bank of the Esk on the road marked Penton. We looked along the river for either heron or cormorants and were rewarded by one statuesque jenny heron standing in the shallows waiting for her dinner to swim past. After about half a mile, the road left the river and we turned up a path through the wood on our left. Since writing, most of this wood has been clear felled but to make matters easy for us the path was indicated by a cairn. As we walked up through the wood we could hear the raucous calls from a heronry in the treetops; oft-times I have seen heron families in a little pond in the adjacent field.

At the top of this wood we came to the track of a disused railway line, on the other side of which the path continued as we followed it through a grove of sessile oaks and alongside a deep, steep cleuch almost choked with scrub willows. This place is known as 'Jenny Noble's Gill' where an old lady of that name is reputed to have committed suicide by hanging herself. About two hundred yards later we reached a cart track and duly turned right, following it for half a mile to Broomholmshiels Farm and a macadamised road where we turned left.

The Tarras Water

After crossing a cattle grid we came to the end of a spruce wood on our right. This was the start of the muirland walking, and as we followed the left hand edge of the wood the ground became muddy in places, but as we passed through the birches and alders it soon dried and we were down on the banks of the Tarras. We were now in the first of two 'Beef Tubs' where the Reivers of four hundred years ago hid the stolen English (or Scottish) cattle. Just before the end of the clearing we looked across the burn at the stratified coal seams on an eroded cliff, an outcrop of the old Canonbie coalfield.

On this side of the Tarras a continuation of the cliff formed an obstacle which we overcame at low water by scrambling around it; at times of high water I have had to climb the steep banking, to find an ancient reiver's larach on top. Once around we were into another hidden valley where a new strong footbridge gives access to the opposite bank of the Tarras. At the other end of this clearing the route along the river was barred by bracken and birches so we climbed up the banking, out of the beef tub and onto the muir. We turned left along the muir road and stayed on it until we returned to Langholm.

The old railway track

As an alternative, at the Skipper's Bridge we could have continued along the Penton road until in two miles at the bottom of a steep hill we crossed a bridge over the Tarras and immediately turned left, following the river for a mile until the above footbridge is reached. Once across this bridge the original route is resumed out of the beef tub and onto the muir.

5: OUT TO CRUMPTON

This walk is about 11 miles and is almost all on hill ground. From the Kilngreen we crossed the Langholm Bridge and at the Primary School turned left onto Eskdaill Street until, opposite the telephone box, we turned up a rough lane known as Jamie's Brae. Corrie and I continued climbing this road until we reached the gate onto Meikleholm Hill. In season this is a magical panoply of yellow rattle, tormentil, trefoil or ragwort, of white yarrow, sneezewort or eyebright, of pink campion or ragged robin, or of multi-coloured orchids. But I always take care around any calving Galloway cattle during the month of April! The gradient became a little steeper as we passed a water reservoir/tank on the right, and whenever we treated ourselves to a wee rest the Border countryside gradually unfolded. To the south in the Lakeland Hills, Skiddaw and Blencatra were prominent, with the Solway Firth, Criffel, Queensberry and the Galloway Hills to the west.

The hillside becomes an Alpine meadow in summer when thousands of flowers await their turn to change the landscape to blue, yellow or pink. Just beyond the top of Meikleholm we reached a gate in the dyke and so on to the top of Timpen. The name is confusing because this hill, locally known as Timpen, is marked on OS maps as Mid Hill, while Timpen is shown nearly a mile further on.

Looking north through the 'Gates of Eden'

Fingland

Just across Eskdale, I could see our return journey from Crumpton with its horseshoe of spruce trees leading down to Douglen and then along the gentle ridge of Potholm and Castle Hills. But back on this side of Eskdale we followed the fence then the dyke round to Craig Hill, keeping a lookout for the rare Grass of Parnassus. Due north of Craig Hill we descended to an ancient larach of a hill fort sitting on top of a steep rise and continued down an equally ancient but barely discernible grassy track towards the Westerkirk road.

We turned left for about 200 yards to where a road signposted for Hawick branched down to the right. At Burnfoot Bridge we turned left along an unmade road and took the right fork after a few yards. The large house on our left was the home of the erstwhile parish minister, the Reverend Malcolm, who had 17 of a family (or his poor wife had), four of whom became knighted as Admirals or Generals. Whenever we reach the farm buildings on this walk I always look for the biblical text carved above the cart house: *He causeth the grass to grow for the cattle. And herb for the service of man.* At this point we made a right-handed U-turn and followed the forestry hill road through the wood, at the end of which we were into the Fingland which is derived from the Gaelic 'Fionglen' meaning the Fair Valley. This contrasts with the glen a mile away on the east of the forest called Douglen or the Black Glen.

Once through a couple of gates we followed the edge of the wood almost to the top of Crumpton Hill. But watch for the boggy ground. The last time I was up here I had just warned my companions when I stepped in over my knees. Fortunately nobody noticed and I never said a word! On the way up we had heard buzzards and kestrels but had no luck with the golden eagles which have been known to nest in these glens.

From Crumpton Hill, we looked north up Teviotdale to Hawick and the Eildons before turning back south along the fence. The view encompasses most of Sir Walter Scott's 'Blue Bonnets' country as well as the Lakes, Solway Firth and parts of Galloway:

March, march, Ettrick and Teviotdale, why m'lads dinna ye march forward in order
March, march, Eskdale and Liddesdale, all the Blue Bonnets are over the Border.

From the corner of the forest we continued downhill, passing the Addergill where there often are adders. At the bealach or saddle where the forest ends, we went uphill along the fence to the Bauchle Hill. This should read Buachaille Hill on the OS map and is Gaelic for Hill of the Herdsman.

We then headed due south to meet the Mill Burn and crossed the road through the gate to a farm track which we followed for half a mile to a line of trees where we turned left through another gate. We followed the fence uphill for half a mile to the Wrae Hass or pass. Turning right, through a gate, we walked past the stumps of an ancient wood and along the ridge of Potholm Hill where near the top we crossed a linear earthworks about 300 yards long.

After we passed the cairn it was downhill almost all the way to Langholm. From the top of Castle Hill the panoramic view to the Lake District and the Solway was worth all our efforts; but closer at hand I counted 18 ancient larachs or earthworks, most of them down towards the valley bottom but some quite high up on the hillside.

6: JOCK'S HOPE AND THE LADY FLORANCE STONE

This walk starts and ends six miles north of Langholm on the Hawick road at the lay-by in front of the Bush Farm. The walk, a mixture of track and heather, is seven miles long and involves a climb of about 2000 feet. It can be combined with the Mosspeeble walk, giving a total of 13 miles (see Chapter 18).

We went over the cattle grid on the right of the farm entrance. A second grid took us onto the track which we were to follow up the valley as far as Rigfoot. The Belstane Rig which rises between Wolf Hope and Jock's Hope was really quite a gentle climb before it levelled off, but with the steep slope to Roughbank Height still rising beyond. However, our immediate objective lay right beside us; a 'village' of eight rectangular larachs, each about 15 yards by 5 yards with an open 'horn' curving out from one of the narrow ends; obviously a 'kep' to direct the animals into their part of the enclosure. The smaller part would be the family's living quarters.

We walked due north from the larachs and then down the steep slope to Burngrains (OS79 366939) at the entrance to Jock's Hope. From there the forestry road climbed

The Lady Florance Stone

The rare Grass of Parnassus

inexorably onwards but we left it after a mile and turned south-west at the second sheepfauld where a post directed us into the Thacky Sike (OS79 355945). By now the sun had disappeared and we were enveloped in a damp grey mist. There was no need for a compass because the sike is narrow and deep.

Eventually, as we gained height, the sides fell away and we were on the open muir, completely enveloped in mist. Having resorted to compass and map to walk due south we felt the ground slowly fall away and as we dropped out of the clouds a new burn began to take shape. I was relieved to find that we were in Wolf Hope.

As we walked a short distance down the path the sun began to reappear and I kept looking up the right hand slope until I saw a stone slab on the skyline. It was only about 200 metres above us but the slope was inexorably steep. We left the path and eventually found a headstone complete with inscription commemorating the fact that the rather silly Lady Florance Custs from Belton House in Lincolnshire had ridden her horse straight down the drop. And she did not even ask what the horse felt about it! Lady Florance had been on her honeymoon at the time, so she may perhaps have had her mind on other things.

While up there we found innumerable cloudberries with their yellow fruits, but already a touch of frost had tinted the bronze and green leaves with gold and silver. In the autumn I have often found Grass of Parnassus on these slopes. Then we were up on top of Longgrain Head from where we could see the Wisp and Tudhope Hill to the north and Maiden Paps to the east. To the south lay the Pennines and Lakeland and the Solway Firth.

Our route lay due east to Stake Hill, where a 120 degree turn and one mile of walking took us sharply down to Brieryshaw Hill. This was the highlight of our walk, as it is the site of the remarkable larach of an ancient fort with three lines of defence and a ditch still visible as well as the foundations of numerous buildings within the enclosure. Right in the centre of the fortification were two cows, but as we approached I realised that one of the cows was in fact a bull - rather a large bull, and it was interested in the dog! Fortunately, we were able to make our escape without incident.

Incidentally, Eskdale and Ewesdale have a total of 369 recorded archaeological sites; one of the greatest concentrations remaining in the whole of Scotland. The Bush Farm lay only half a mile away to the north.

7: WARBLA

We started this six-mile walk at the Kilngreen, and after crossing the Langholm Bridge, turned left into Elizabeth Street, at the end of which we turned right as far as the footbridge into Buccleuch Park. We walked across the park, passing the award-winning war memorial and the adjacent playpark. The path continued along the bank of the Esk, through masses of snowdrops, daffodils, primroses and wild hyacinths each in their own season. At the Skipper's Bridge we turned right along the main road for a short distance before turning right up a path through the woods and so onto a rough track. We walked along the lip of the deep Skipper's Cleuch until just before two cottages we turned left through a metal gate.

This track past Mouldy Hills took us along the dyke at the top of the wood until we reached Middleholm (pronounced Midlum) and a deep cleuch down through the Dean Banks wood. This cleuch is called Gaber Gill, which is probably a corruption of the Gaelic *gabhar* meaning a goat; 'Goat Gill' would certainly fit with the terrain. By now the track had deteriorated into a quad-bike route and then a sheep trod before we went through a gate at the head of Gaber Gill and onto the open hillside.

From the gate it was only a quarter-mile south-west onto Burian Hill, where I hoped to see one of three bloomeries known to be on this muir. You may be wondering what a

Langholm and Whita Hill from Warbla

Potholm and Castle Hill from Warbla

bloomery is. Two thousand years ago, primitive iron, which bears little relation to the modern metal, was made by smelting iron ore on mounds of earth using vast amounts of timber. The resulting 'blooms' of very impure metal were hammered into shape when still hot. I found one such bloomery on the east side of the small Burian Hill – but there was really very little to see.

From there we walked on a bearing of 330 degrees, and soon Warbla came into view across the empty open muir. All of a sudden a man and a dog took shape less than 100 yards away; they must have been walking in a slight hollow hidden from us. The odd thing was, we were on a direct collision course on this flat plain. If we had been driving cars there would have been a frightful crash.

From the summit of Warbla, the panorama is wide; the Pennines, the Lake District, the Solway with perhaps the Isle of Man on a clear day. As our eyes traversed the horizon past Criffel, Queensberry and the Lowther Hills hove into view in the north-west, while still going clockwise we could see the Moffat Hills and Ettrick Pen. Before us as we looked down into Liddesdale, Eskdale and Annandale we could see almost the whole of the Debateable Lands to the south. Beneath us Eskdale was ablaze with glorious vibrant autumnal colour; browns and golds, yellows and ambers, reds and greens.

The name Warbla (or Warb Law or Ward Law) means a Beacon Hill, and is common in Scotland. From the mast on top of Warbla a good track took us down the northern side, returning to Langholm through the Buccleuch Park.

8: PIKE FELL AND UNTHANK PIKES

This fairly strenuous walk consists of about 14.5 miles of track and hill walking and should take about six hours.

We turned off the A7 Hawick road at Fiddleton Toll and parked at the cattle grid just before Glenrief Cottage (OS79 395965). There should be ample space where marked, without blocking the gate to the hill track.

Once onto the hillside there is in season, a glorious display of primroses or todtails (foxgloves). After a mile the slope eased off and I stopped to admire the scenery. In fact it was really to get my breath back, but I didn't let on to the dog. I kept an eye open for roedeer as there are a few in the surrounding hills and woods. Just past the gate into the forest the track divided; we could have taken either way, but the left-hand branch high above the windy pass to Mosspaul is probably the more interesting when going north.

We gradually climbed until we looked down onto the Mosspaul Inn; not too far away to dissuade any drouthy walkers. There was a clear panorama down Teviotdale towards Hawick, the Eildons and the Lammermuirs. And so we went on, up and east, surrounded

Tudhope Hill

Pike Fell and Unthank Pikes from Salter Grain

by spruces. By now we had a vista of friendly but steep hills; Wisp, Tudhope, Pennygant with Maiden Pap away in the east. It was late summer so I looked among the heather for the rare cloudberries or Queensberries with their single white flower and orange bramble-like fruit. I found one; it was tasteless!

Once again the track divided. The right branch is an 'easy out' back down Glenrief into the panorama of Ewesdale, Solway and Lakeland. However, we followed the lower track into Penangus Hope until the track became a grassy ride through the spruce trees. By the side of the route was a fire lookout post with a burn across our path.

This ride came out at the end of the wood after 300 yards, whereupon a sunny mist seemed to come from nowhere. We took a compass bearing of 45 degrees and headed for Little Tudhope. This involved a drop of 135 metres into Carewoodrig Hope, pronounced Carrotrig. Fortunately the mist was short-lived, but unfortunately this descent was followed by a climb of 225 metres onto Tudhope Hill from where it was a straightforward walk on a bearing of 160 degrees down to the Hermitage road. At this point we could have turned down the road to Carewoodrig and the car, giving an eight-mile walk.

We were no sooner down and across the road than we had to climb back up to Geordie's Hill, then followed a mile of easy walking south-west to Tamond Heights. There could be an escape route, almost due west to Butter Hill and the road. On Butter Hill there is a small upright slab with runic-like scratchings upon it. It does not appear to have religious connotations, but could it have been a method of counting sheep?

From Tamond Heights, at a bearing of 200 degrees, it is an easy mile and a half to Pike Fell, from where four glens seemed to start right at our feet; Tarras, Twistlehope, Mosspeeble and Unthank. Just to the south we could see the nick of the 'Bloody Cleuch' on Mosspeeble Burn. Five hundred years ago, when the Border Reivers were secure in their impenetrable Tarras hideaway, a raiding party planned to come out by this route. But they were betrayed to the Dragoons who ambushed them in the Bloody Cleuch. All the Reivers were killed and to this day the burn still floods red with blood. A fine tale, but in fact the top of this Bloody Cleuch Linn consists of red boulder clay or keelstane; hence the blood-red flood colour.

From Unthank Pikes we went carefully down the steep wet slope to the north-west. After wet weather this shank becomes messy with sliding slabs of grass and moss. However we soon reached the Unthank track and followed it to the farm. Just to the right of the farm there is a knowe on which a much earlier settlement had been built. Traces of even older buildings lie underneath. Then at the farm itself is the ancient larach of the Over Kirk of Ewes, abandoned at the Reformation. Incidentally, Unthank means a forest clearing, inhabited by squatters.

The final part of our walk was a mile and a bittock along the main A7 road to Fiddleton Toll, to Burnfoot and finally back to Glenrief.

9: ETTRICK PEN

At 2270 feet, Ettrick Pen is not particularly high and although steep in places it is not particularly difficult; the walk is about ten miles in length and should take about four and a half hours, with half of the walk being on forestry roads and the remainder on the open hill. As a reward it has an extremely wide panorama from the top. I had not been on 'The Pen' since the ubiquitous spruce trees had grown tall but I had promised the dog that we would go there one of these days. And that day had come!

It is 13 miles from Langholm to Eskdalemuir and another two miles to Garwald Waterfoot where we visited the Samye Ling Buddhist Centre before driving up the Garwald Burn. Garwald is a corruption of the Gaelic *garbh allt* meaning 'rough water' and both river and road certainly lived up to the name as we stopped to look into the deep ravine at the rocks, the raging water and the plethora of wild flowers.

We passed the 'ferm toon' of Garwald and entered the forest where we were to remain for some miles. Even though we were among the trees, the draw of Ettrick Pen was before us for most of the way, with the river beside us. There are still a few cottages within the Eskdalemuir Forest, now alas the majority are holiday homes or are empty. But the first house we came to was occupied; Ashy Bank even had a sign outside advertising 'Free Range Eggs', although it rather looked like 'Free - Range Eggs'. There was another sign saying 'Dead - Slow Children'. However, we declined the offer.

Kiddamhill lay another mile further up this rough road; a snod wee farm with a flower-filled garden, but most of the farm land had been gobbled up by the ever-encroaching forest. A stranger had recently arrived at Kiddamhill looking rather weary. His first words to the farmer were, "Where am I?" He had been walking west on the Southern Upland Way and everything had gone well until he reached Ettrick Head where the track ended. And so did his luck! Instead of bearing south-west to Moffat he had kept on due south to end up five miles later at Kiddamhill. His next words were; "Where can I get a bus to Moffat?" Not much chance of that here.

We parked the car just before the farm and walked down a rough track to the right as far as the cottage of Thickside, just beyond which we met up with another forestry road and turned left to cross a concrete bridge over the Garwald Burn. We immediately turned right and followed the west bank of the river. It was rough walking for a quarter-mile along a brashed path, but we crossed the Powmuck Burn and almost immediately met the end of another forest road. At normal water, this small burn can be stepped across, but after a wet spell, walkers should be prepared to wade. In dry weather we could have followed the other side of the Garwald Water and boulder-hopped across the burn at this point.

We followed the new road for a mile and crossed a bridge to a corrugated iron barn at one end of a long clearing, with the substantial cottage of Pengrains at the other. But our route led us up to the left at the next fork and well above Pengrains until in a mile we came to a U-bend where the track turned back down the other side of the valley. At this juncture, the West Burn, the source of the Garwald, cuts across the road. We followed this wee burn a short distance to the open hillside. Ettrick Pen was then only a steep half mile away to the north east.

Both Corrie and I were glad to be out of the trees and to see some wide sky! The panorama was well worth the effort; especially across the Ettrick Valley and Moffat Water to the hills of White Coomb and Hart Fell. The Solway and the Galloway Hills lay to the south-west with Queensberry further away. The radar masts on the Lowther Hills were outlined against the windy sky, while in the north the triple peaks of the Eildons and The Cheviot could be spied in a wet haze.

After admiring the view from the cairn on Ettrick Pen, we turned back along the fence to the south-west for a mile to Hopetoun Craig and then another mile to Wind Fell. With the fence on our right, we climbed onto the 2257ft Loch Fell (OS79 170048). Although these hills are all about the same height, there is a deep bealach or saddle between each one. From the trig point on Loch Fell we dropped a steep 450 feet to meet a track at the head of Dryfesdale. We turned left along this road to re-enter the forest where, ignoring any side roads, we were back at Kiddamhill in another three miles.

10: TARGET BURN AND WHITA HILL

This is a rough woodland and muirland walk of some four miles and should take less than two hours. Corrie, my black labrador, and I walked north out of Langholm, past the Kilngreen and as far as the High Mill Brig with its traffic lights where we took the track to the right along the banks of the Ewes Water. At various seasons this area is a 'colourama' of wild flowers such as snowdrops, coltsfoot, wild daffodils, campion, willowherb and many more. Further along the river we came to a small clearing where we looked around for any evidence from which the name 'Target Burn' was derived. There was very little apart from some long forgotten and crumbling structures about four feet high and lined with red rusted steel plates. Over this wall and hidden in some dense undergrowth of willows was an equally red rusted metal footbridge spanning the Ewes.

These are the remains of a rifle range from the times of the Boer War and later the First and Second World Wars and would have been used by Territorial Soldiers. The deep cleuch is now known locally as the Target Burn but is shown on the OS map as Far Whitshiels Cleuch.

We followed the track round a corner and over a deep cundy until it ended in a turning area. The burn now lay down on our left and looking across I could see, about twenty metres downstream, a quad bike track climbing through a mass of wild hyacinths (or bluebells) to the brow of the hill. At that point we turned right and followed the fence and then a drystane dyke until we came to a fixed gate. Once over this and onto the muir we followed the dyke along the edge of the wood and through two small cleuchs, the second of which was lined with willow trees.

By now we were crossing the Whitshiels Bog where in season I

The MacDiarmid Memorial

have found such plants as milkwort, gentian, asphodel, orchids and mushrooms. We knew that a bull normally ran with the cows during the summer on the Moss but by holding to the dyke it was easy to avoid any trouble. We followed the dyke as it went uphill over steep, rough ground until we reached the Newcastleton road and then walked up it as far as the MacDiarmid Memorial, which is in the form of a huge open book made from Corten steel and bronze. At this point we spent some time in contemplation of lovely Ewesdale.

MacDiarmid is frequently depicted as always writing in broad Scots, being too long-winded or being too profound. But he has also written many quite emotionally beautiful short verses such as:

The Malcolm Monument

The rose of all the world is not for me,
I want for my part
Only the little white rose of Scotland
That smells sharp and sweet - and breaks the heart

From the MacDiarmid memorial it was less than a mile up the broad track to the Malcolm Monument, the more obvious obelisk on top of Whita Hill. The view had undergone a transformation to the south, where we could now see a panorama from the Pennines to the Ribble Gorge, the complete Lake District from east to west and across the Solway Firth to the Galloway hills.

The path down to Langholm was now obvious. On the way down we looked for - and found - the Soldier's Head on the side of the path. Before going down the Whita Road, past the Golf Course and back to Langholm we had a drink of real water from the Whita Well and appreciated the closer scenery from the seat.

11: POTHOLM AND CASTLE HILLS

This is a six-mile (10km) walk in forest and on the hill and should take no more than three hours. The outward section is the same as for the Langfauld and Potholm walk (Chapter 7).

As we approached the northern end of the Langfauld wood the road began to make its descent to Potholm Farm and farmhouse, where we turned sharp right and back uphill to the line of the original road. This detour had been necessary to avoid the deep Potholm Cleuch where a once substantial masonry bridge had become unsafe and had been dismantled. We turned left for only about 100 metres before passing through a gate on our right from where we followed a fence uphill to the ridge or Wrae Hass, which is old Norse for 'a corner of good land on a pass'. At that point we went through a gate leading to a small clump of five blasted trees.

The remains of a long since felled wood were very evident in the form of moss-covered tree stumps, but the most interesting artefact on this Wrae Hass was an old road which seemed to drop down from the Wrae Hill to the north and back up the Potholm Hill to

Warbla from Castle Hill

the south. Following the ridge south, up and over an ancient lineal earthworks, we reached the top of Potholm Hill.

We walked alongside the remains of a dyke, the stones of which had been used to build a large cairn overlooking both the Esk and the Ewes. I once counted 18 ancient forts or settlements which could be seen from this belvedere, and there are many more just out of sight. But further afield and more scenic are the Solway and its surrounding hills; Scafell, Skiddaw and Helvellyn on the English side with Criffel, Queensberry and the Cairnmores on the Scottish side.

We kept on alongside the ruined dyke before passing through a gate. Then, on top of the Castle Hill, the dyke turned sharp left to descend into Ewesdale, but we continued straight on until Langholm came into sight. If I am crossing the Castle Hill during April or May I always keep an eye open for calving black Galloways as they can be a bit obstreperous if disturbed; and sometimes when they have not been disturbed. The town was still well below us, but we managed to intersect a new hill track which gave us easy walking down to Pathhead and so back across the Ewes Bridge to Langholm.

12: ARKLETON CRAIGS

Although this walk is only seven miles long it has many interesting features. Much of the walk is on hill tracks but stout footwear will be required.

We left the car in a convenient lay-by four miles north of Langholm on the main A7 Hawick road and walked down the private drive towards Arkleton House. It is an interesting shape, but later from the top of the hill we were to see it from quite a different perspective. Before reaching the house we crossed the bridge to the farmyard, and continued on up the hill track past some cottages to an area of ground with evidence of ancient earthworks. At the end of the wood the track divided and we took the right hand uphill route over Bittleston Shank and on upwards until the road entered the spruce plantation on Auldshiels Hill (OS79 399905) from where we could see Arkleton House as it was originally planned; a typical Border Keep with some later buildings attached.

Immediately before the forest gate we turned north (left) for about a mile to the top of Arkleton Hill where we turned west down along a fence then a drystane dyke to the bottom of the Arkleton Craigs. On the way downhill, the Arkleton Lochan was in front of us, beyond a line of trees. This is a favourite area for the herds of wild goats common

Twin waterfalls on the track above Arkleton

Arkleton Hill

to these hills, while in the sky we often manage a sighting of peregrines or ravens. There is reputed to be a cave called Lady Boodle's Cave somewhere among the rocks but I have never found it; nor to my knowledge has anyone else! Incidentally, boodle means spoil or money obtained by corruption, while a boddle was an old copper coin.

We continued south along the track until in half a mile I looked across the Birren Sike to where a very obvious prehistoric circular settlement occupied the middle of the Birren (Burial) Rig. Corrie and I went across to investigate and tried to imagine the area as it might have been, thousands of years ago. From there it was only half a mile back down the track to Arkleton Farm.

13: THE BECKS

I used only to take this 3-mile walk in dry weather or resorted to my wellies as the small Becks Burn had to be be forded. Now, however, there is a fine new footbridge across it, so the walk can be enjoyed regardless of the conditions.

We left the Kilngreen and turned right to cross the Langholm Bridge into Thomas Telford Road, turning left past the Academy into Eskdaill Street. Opposite a telephone box we turned right into a rough lane known as Jamie's Brae which was the start of the ancient route up Wauchopedale to Dumfries and on into Galloway. We continued climbing up this rough road past some houses until we reached a small open area at a crossroads, from where we walked along behind the wood for half a mile until the track deteriorated into a grassy path leading down to the Becks Burn. During May and June this whole track is a mass of wild flowers. I have counted as many as 68 different varieties on a single day.

We crossed the burn at the new footbridge (not the Red Banking). A steep but short climb up some steps and then along a path led us in 200 metres to the Becks road where we turned left. Just past a new house we looked over the hedge on our right to where the mounds of the old Wauchope Castle can be traced as it straddles the Lockerbie Road.

The track leading out from Langholm

WALKING WITH WANDERER

The suspension bridge over the Esk in Langholm

The castle was built by Sir John Lindsay around 1258 when the family was granted the land by King Alexander III. In 1518 the old fortifications became the property of Lord Maxwell, the Warden of the Western Marches, but it was not until 1549 that he started to rebuild the castle. However, by 1662 it was marked as a ruin on Blaeu's map.

Down at the T-junction we turned right through the larachs of the castle to cross the 'Auld Stane Brig' where we turned immediately left through the gate onto Gaskell's Walk. This maintained path follows the deep cleuch, through which the Wauchope Water ferociously tumbles in wet weather.

We looked for tiny goldcrests and siskins on the conifer trees until, near the end of the woodland path, we crossed the Bogle Gill, but we saw neither birds nor ghosts. We passed Stubholm, the erstwhile home of that likeable rogue Archie Armstrong. Archie was a freebooter and sheep-stealer who, after one of his thieving expeditions, managed to get back to Stubholm and placed the body of the sheep into the bairn's cradle. Sadly for him, it was discovered, and as the Royal Court was in the area, he was taken before King James IV and condemned to death. But the lad managed to joke his way out of the sentence – and the King appointed him court jester.

At Stubholm we turned right along the loaning and followed the track along the wood and eventually down to the river where we turned left through the Beechy Plains with its masses of wild hyacinths and primroses in season. And so back into the Buccleuch Park and Langholm.

14: CALKIN AND BOYKENHOPEHEAD

This is an easy eight-mile walk, almost all on forestry roads, beginning and ending at the Boyken road end (OS79 318888) just south of Bentpath, locally known as 'The Benty'. We parked and walked up the farm road past Old Hopsrigg and over a number of sikes, frequented by many different birds such as mistle thrushes, herons and buzzards. Just before we reached the spruce wood which straddles the road we skirted the larach of a prehistoric settlement; in fact there were three such circles stretching across the valley at this point, like some prehistoric barrier. I could have brought the car as far as this point, thus reducing the walk by two miles but missing out a lovely pastoral stroll above the Boyken Burn.

This small valley rises onto the muir before the ground falls away into the Milk Valley and at one time the road was used as a local drove road. The story goes that a young shepherd called Wull Bell was driving a score of his master's sheep from the market at Langholm to the Milk Valley. It grew dark but the dogs knew the way. Eventually in the early morning they arrived at the farm, but it seemed to take a long time to drive the sheep into the field. Finally Wull got to bed in the bothy, only to be wakened by the farmer's wife shouting that there were "thoosans o' sheep in the yaird". The dogs had

Looking west from Calkin

Footbridge over the Hole Sike

collected all the sheep they could find on the dark hillsides and brought them home!

The next place we came to was the lonely cottage of Calkin sitting down in the bottom of the glen. Just past Calkin we took the high road and two miles further on, looked down on the cottage of Boykenhopehead. Like many other shepherds' cottages they both lie empty and forlorn; a testament to the invention of the All Terrain Vehicle or quad bike. On one occasion at this point I watched a dotterel, it was quite unperturbed. At first the views were fairly local across to Crumpton and Douglen Hills but as we climbed, the vista to the western Solway expanded until it encompassed the entire horizon from Criffel round the Galloway hills to Queensberry, the Lowther and the Moffat Hills as well as Annandale and Nithsdale.

From our viewpoint we had a choice of going down to the empty cottage at Boykenhopehead, but I had had a surfeit of looking through the sad windows of empty cottages, so we followed the winding track back along the opposite side of the valley where it undulated into the cleuchs and over the knowes until it came to an abrupt end. We were only about 200 yards along a rough path to the edge of the forest, where we followed the fence down the rough steep hillside and so back to the original lower track alongside the burn.

On the higher muirlands of the Boyken we had seen a pair of buzzards. Three kestrels were hovering over the lower slopes while down by the burnside we disturbed a ring ouzel at its nest, and a dipper was furiously flying up the water before turning at the end of its 'beat' to fly back down again.

15: THE CRAIG BURN

You can walk for miles in the Borders and never see a soul. Even quite close to houses, the countryside can appear to be deserted. Much depends on the weather, but even on the brightest of days, we still meet the same old faces, until I even begin to recognise the dogs and the dogs start to recognise me. Perhaps it has something to do with the dog biscuits in my pocket!

It was a glorious morning as I parked the car nearly opposite The Craig farm at double field gates, being careful not to block either of them. We climbed up the initially steep slope on the left of the fence until, after it levelled off, a path branched off back to the left and climbed on up the hill. This man-made path is obviously of considerable antiquity; four hundred or four thousand years, I cannot tell, but I can feel and almost visualise the line of slaves as they laboured up the slope with supplies of food and water for the signal station or fort.

Like the slaves, we passed through a cleft in what could have been the outer defences. And so to the top, where little remained of the fort except masses of crumbled boulders

Looking north from the old settlement on Craig Hill

contained within the ruin of an inner wall, while an outer wall and a deep ditch surrounded everything. The remnants of five large contemporary cairns completed the picture.

The Craig Hill stood due south of us, but we descended south-west, round a small shelterbelt wood and into Glenbeg, where we turned left onto the track which took us round Torbeck Hill to a sharp hairpin bend. But we carried on along an old, boggy and overgrown track until we came to a morass of rushes and sphagnum from which Glencorf Burn flows south and the Craig Burn flows north. In the middle of this bog, a boulder rose out of the mosses. It seems to have become smaller over the years, but perhaps the vegetation is rising. This stone is reputed to mark the site of the duel between two members of the Beattie Clan as described in chapter 19, Glencorf and the Becks. Incidentally, Glencorf means 'glen of the memorial'.

Back at the track, we looked for the remains of an old house or sheiling, but could not find much, although there is an area of flat, enclosed ground right next to the burn. From there it was downhill all the way along the other side of the Craig Burn. From over the top of the brae on our left, I could make out the tops of the trees in the Arresgill Forest as they peeped with disdain down into our glen at the small shelterbelts. From the large forests, buzzards and other raptors have frequently been seen searching for prey.

As we descended, Westerkirk, the birthplace of Thomas Telford, was in the foreground ahead of us, with Crumpton Hill beyond. We walked on, passing through a number of gates until we reached the 'ferm toon' of Carlesgill. Soon we were back to the road at Kemra before returning to the car at The Craig.

16: TARRAS LODGE TO PERTERBURN

As only a short nature walk was the order of the day, we left the car at Tom's Seat, just up the glen from Tarras Lodge, about midway between Newcastleton and Langholm. The late Tom Irving was probably the most knowledgeable person on local birds that I have ever met. He loved to sit in this favoured spot for hours on end; as Tom repeatedly said to me "You walk about far ower much to see birds – sit down for a minute!"

Ignoring those wise words, Corrie and I walked back uphill towards Langholm as far as the Middlemoss track. On the way through the alder and birch trees we were looking down into the tree canopies where the last of the flycatchers were darting out from the branches to catch a flying insect before returning to their perches. There were a few long-tailed tits flitting from branch to branch. In spring this is a favourite haunt of cuckoos, and unfortunately adders; although an inquisitive dog is more liable to be bitten on the nose than is a human (on the nose or anywhere else for that matter).

This is one of the most interesting smaller areas in Eskdale, interesting from the abundance of nature, and from the peaceful ambience of this hidden valley. But although short it is far from an easy walk. The main interest on this walk lies in the solitude and peace and the diversity of terrain. But on the return journey, this very terrain has created one of the toughest bits of walking anywhere in the area and although short and beautiful, strong footwear is essential – this one is definitely not recommended for Great Auntie and her stiletto heels!

Deep in the Tarras Water woods

WALKING WITH WANDERER

We followed the track for a mile and a bittock, past Middlemoss and so downhill to the Perterburn ford. During a dry spell the burn is easily crossed on foot at this point, "but the water was wide and we could not get over". So, nothing daunted, we turned downstream and it was only about 300 yards to a substantial footbridge hidden away among the trees. I was following Corrie through the low trees and, forgetting that I was a wee bit taller than he, I nearly felled myself on a low branch. By this time I had changed my mind, so we did not cross the river but followed a waymarker back to Middlemoss, from where we made our way back down to the river, but further upstream opposite the Perter Burn.

There was no hurry, so we took our time to search for lizards among the heather and rocks of the riverbank and listened for the kitten-like calls of the buzzards or harriers as they scoured the muir. After only about five minutes we were lucky and even surprised to get a look at a wee brown lizard basking in what could have been one of the last days of warm summer sunshine. Soon the lizard would have to look for a sheltered crack or crevice under a stone in which to hibernate. I think it had an orange-coloured underside, so it was probably a male.

Then we were into the old birch and alder trees where the sides of the valley grew steeper and the valley grew deeper. Some trees had fallen, taking the banking with them and making it difficult to cross. Soon both Corrie and the Wanderer had a coating of red glaur, and it was by no means superficial! However, we reached a small burn as it tumbled over the rocks to join the Tarras; as we stopped I looked up, and there in the high crotch of an old oak tree was a dark shadow. It was a long-eared owl. Being nocturnal, it merely looked at us with its big orange eyes, decided we were innocuous and went back to sleep.

We luxuriated in the damp green mossy silence, broken only by the burble of the Tarras as it flowed, sometimes slowly, usually rapidly to the Esk. Further upstream the river became deeper and broader as it skirted a beef-tub where the grass grew greener as if cropped by sheep, as indeed it was. A grey wagtail was bob-bob-bobbing on a rock in midstream, while below us a dipper patrolled its beat, up and down the pool.

We reluctantly left this pleasant place and entered the realm of large rocks, waterfalls and deep pools where it seemed to get warmer. So below Charlie's Planting we sat and watched as a black mink spied a wee rabbit, and chased it among the rocks at furious speed. We did not see the result of the chase as the unfortunate prey disappeared into a crevice with the mink in hot pursuit. But an aggressive mink is seldom unsuccessful. From that point it was an easy half-mile past the waterfalls back to Tarras Lodge.

17: THE LANGFAULD AND POTHOLM

This is an easy and pleasant five-mile walk. We walked north from the Town Hall, past the Kilngreen and across the Ewes Bridge with the ruins of Langholm Castle on the left. Johnnie Armstrong of Gilnockie was the leader of the Armstrong clan and was keeper of Langholm Castle. Like so many other reivers he was not averse to skullduggery and mayhem; indeed, he was a thorn in the side to both the English and the Scottish kings. He and some of his followers were invited "lovingly" by King James V to a friendly meeting at Carlinrig in Teviotdale. The 50 unarmed Armstrongs were greeted by 8000 of the King's men, and all 50 were hanged.

We walked on along the Lodge Walk through some magnificent hemlock trees. On our left we passed the converted Langholm Lodge, which had been the Eskdale mansion of the Dukes of Buccleuch. The right-hand fork led us through the woods to Holmhead and round the steading to where the road continued to the North Lodge.
At this point we went through the gate in the policy walls and into the Langfauld Woods which are amenity woodlands of mixed spruce, silver fir, Scots pine, hemlock and Douglas as well as virtually all the hardwoods that can be grown in Scotland. Throughout the woods can be found large areas of rhododendrons and azaleas.

The road continued high above the Esk until in a mile it dropped to Potholm Farm. I often make a small diversion past the steading to Staplegordon Cemetery and the larach of Barntalloch Castle. Like many other place names in Eskdale, this is of Gaelic origin and means 'Hill of the Forges'. We crossed the bridge over the Esk and continued back towards Langholm on the farm road, passing on our right two prehistoric settlements, especially obvious when the sun is low.

A mile later, just before the farm road joins the road from Langholm to Eskdalemuir, we made an interesting and attractive diversion as indicated by a signpost. This took us through the wall and down onto an old woodland path, hardly used, it seems, since the demise of Langholm Lodge half a century ago.

The path is now being restored, and it led us gradually down through fine mixed woodland to the banks of the Esk. In time we reached the Duchess Bridge, a graceful span which was the first cast-iron bridge in Scotland and when erected in 1813, to a design by William Keir, drew a great deal of attention. It is worth pausing here to look up and down river. The views themselves are lovely and birds you may see include heron, dippers and gulls. Past the bridge, we were soon back to the road and the final walk into Langholm.

18: MOSSPEEBLE AND BLOODY GILL

This walk consists of hill track and heather and is about seven miles long, climbing about 400 metres with a start and finish at Mosspeeble Farm. It could be combined with the Lady Florance Stone walk from The Bush, giving a total of 13 miles.

There is ample parking space in a lay-by (OS79 379935) on the west of the Hawick road just south of Mosspeeble road end. At Mosspeeble Farm we followed the road round to the left and crossed the bridge before climbing up to the cottage. As this house was built on part of an ancient settlement and grave site it must surely be haunted, but a lot more can be seen of this oval larach from higher up. We left the settlement and its barking dogs and continued up the main track until it split, with one branch going down to the burn and the other continuing uphill. We could have chosen either way as the route is circular, but I chose to go down to the burn. However, this arrangement was only a short-term easement, as our route was ever upwards.

I kept an eye open for wildlife, hoping to see some evidence of birds of prey such as buzzards, peregrines, ravens and harriers, but it was a bit too warm for them. I could hear the 'peiou-peiou' of four buzzards as they soared high in the sky. At first, as they

A beautiful group of purple foxgloves

were very high, they resembled eagles but the smaller size and head hunched between the shoulders indicated a buzzard. As they flew lower the smaller body and shorter wings confirmed our recognition.

At the Long Grain Burn, where the track came to an end, we took to the steep bracken and heather-clad slope until, following the north bank of the Bloody Cleuch, we reached the larachs of a summer sheiling. At this point the dog became somewhat agitated and on looking into the nearby Linns we were surprised and delighted to see a massive golden eagle perched on a rock only twenty feet away! But not for long, with a lazy flick of its giant wings it dropped from its rock and soared away down the glen. In about a minute it had covered the ground we had toiled up for an hour.

The gradient began to ease for a short time until another steep climb took us to the top of the Cleuch and a deep red eroded clay ditch. Some people say that this is the reason the burn runs red every time there is a flood. But others insist that the real reason is that a party of Reivers who had been in the hidden Tarras Valley planned a raid but had been betrayed. The dragoons ambushed and killed all the Reivers. Hence the blood-red colouring.

From there it was only a mile at 210 degrees over the top to the summit of Arkleton Hill. The route across this high moss was interspersed with peat haggs and hollows of sphagnum moss. At one point the dog raised its nose and looked into the distance until at last I also saw a large herd of around thirty wild, or feral goats. We left the high ground and carefully headed north-west through the steep and rocky Arkleton Craigs until we struck Baraman's Cleuch. Around this area can sometimes be found Grass of Parnassus, which in some years can be somewhat erratic. The cleuch guided us to a hill track which rejoined our original route after half a mile. And so back to the farm of Mosspeeble.

19: GLENCORF AND BECKS

This walk is about 12 miles long and is nearly all on hill ground or track. Strong footwear and full hill walking gear are essential.

We left Langholm by a familiar route which we followed over Timpen (Mid Hill) as far as Timpen Sike before crossing the dyke into Glen Beag or the Wee Glen. The track from The Craig through Glencorf to Wauchopedale was only a short distance below; Corrie and I turned left for a mile or so to a U-bend where the road continued back round the other side of the valley while we left it and continued due south through a maze of wee burns called Jock's Grains. Along the side of one of the small burns was a blur of yellow pimpernel which of late has become fairly common in Eskdale. By now the track had deteriorated to a narrow path, but it was still recognisable as the ancient way it indubitably was from Eskdale to Wauchopedale.

The highest point was the watershed of two burns; the Craig Burn and the Glencorf Burn. We had followed the former to where it oozed out of a squelch of sphagnum moss which now seemed to bounce under our weight until a new little burn appeared, flowing

The Glencorf Burn near the abandoned house of Glencorf

Old, gnarled trees at Glencorf

in the opposite direction. Out of the intervening moss and fern a single small rock reared upwards. Now Glencorf is a Gaelic name for the Glen of the Memorial, and I like to think that this small stone which is gradually being submerged by the encroaching moss is just possibly this same memorial to a dastardly deed of some five centuries ago!

During the 14th and 15th centuries, the Beatties or Batys or Battiesons, although a clan of some power were a "right rough and tough lot". In 1455 after the Battle of Arkinholm they were granted lands in Eskdale by the King and soon owned a considerable part of the valley. These Beattie Reivers made peace with the English but fought with everybody else, even raiding as far as Edinburgh. Things eventually reached such a pass that many people of that name were herded together; some were hanged while others were transported to Ireland. This 14th century 'ethnic cleansing' was not unusual in those days; the reiving families of Graham, Bell and Carruthers among others were also 'proscribed as unruly clans'.

A few Beattie families still remained in Eskdale and a dispute arose between the owner of The Burn (now Burnfoot) and his nephew who lived across the Esk in The Boyken. Satisfaction could only be achieved by a duel. The two sides went to the isolated boundary lands. The uncle was killed and the nephew died on his return journey to the Boyken. There must be a moral in there somewhere. Yes, the stone is still there but it is fast being submerged by the ever encroaching moss and peat. Or is it sinking?

We followed the Glencorf burn for about a mile until we reached the last of the alder trees. Almost underneath a power line (OS79 325828) we turned east up the banking and found the old foundations of a long forgotten sheiling. On some older maps a path is shown along here, but it is not shown in the latest editions as the one-time track has virtually disappeared. But our homeward route followed the power line. After half a mile we came to a regular farm track along a line of crab apple trees and continued on familiar ground past The Becks to join the Langholm road near the site of Wauchope Castle, ancestral home of the Lindsays.

20: GLENRIEF

This five-mile walk is all on forest tracks and should take about two hours. However, it is not waymarked.

We turned off the Hawick road (A7) at Fiddleton Toll (signposted for Hermitage) and just before Glenrief Cottage (OS79 395965) parked at the cattle grid in the space provided, going through the gate onto the hill track. In season there is a glorious display of primroses or todtails on this hillside. We kept an eye open for roe deer which can sometimes be seen bounding through the high bracken and over the burns. It is always interesting to count the number of sheep faulds that can be seen from this hillside. These gathering places are also known as stells, buchts, fanks, bields and pens – each farming district seems to have its own name for them. Some years ago I counted 27 around this hill, but the number has decreased as the enveloping spruce trees and bracken grow higher.

About a mile up the track, the first slope eased off and shortly after entering the forestry plantation, the track divided into two. We chose the left-hand branch high over the winding pass to Mosspaul as it is more interesting in that direction where the views are always ahead.

Butter Hill from the road to Hermitage

The elusive (but tasteless) Cloudberry

The track gradually climbed until we were able to look down on Mosspaul Hotel with a clear view down Teviotdale to Hawick, the Eildons, the Moorfoot Hills and the Lammermuirs. From the highest point of the track we had a more immediate vista of friendly but steep hills; Wisp Hill, Tudhope and Pennygant with Maiden Paps further to the east. As it was late summer I looked among the heather for cloudberries; these elusive relatives of the bramble fruits that are only found on high muirs. If you do find some, do not expect a taste treat - they are almost tasteless!

Once again the track divided, the lower one being the route of a much longer walk. We followed the right hand track which is an 'easy out' down Glenrief with its wide panorama of the Lake District and the Solway. It was now downhill nearly all the way with Ewesdale and Eskdale always before us, culminating in the Solway Firth and Skiddaw. We could see the whole length of the beautiful pastoral Ewes Valley as it stretched from Unthank and Mosspeeble right down to Terrona and Whita. Corrie was not particularly impressed with the view as he took one look and jumped straight into a drainage sump full of dubious water.

The rest of the walk was straightforward and before long we were back at the car having enjoyed our outing.

21: PENTON LINNS

Being relatively short, this walk is more for interest than for exercise. We took the B6308 Penton road south from the Skipper's Bridge for about six miles to the Liddel Water and the Border.

The English bank was jealously guarded with boards and barbed wire as well as a sign indicating that we were not welcome. So we came back to the Scottish side. There, a small car park had notices saying that Buccleuch Estates and Dumfries & Galloway Council welcomed walkers to Penton Linns – 'nuff said. Steps had been made and dangerous places bridged or fenced, while muddy stretches had been infilled with gravel or duckboarded over.

About 100 yards from the car park, we strauchled down the steep banking into the deep bed of the Liddel. The rocks were convoluted and broken as they lay in ridges across the river, which had to wriggle and writhe its way through. In some cases these sharp rocks were over 15 feet high and surrounded by smaller and sharper rocks, making the consequences of a fall potentially serious. At one point I had to help the dog over a particularly slippery area, but at other times he was lucky as he merely jumped into the water and swam round the obstacle.

According to my geologist friend Ivor who was with me, the ground had been laid down over millions of years from layers of lime and shale, with sand being washed down on top. Finally, layers of vegetable matter had been washed down and compressed to form coal. This process was repeated many times to form alternating layers.

Then came the great upheavals when Penton Linns was twisted, folded and turned on edge. Ivor pointed out a striking feature in the form of an anticline, which resembles an inverted bowl about 30 feet across and ten feet deep. Under much larger anticlines deep in the earth, gas or oil can be found. He also pointed out fossilised shells, fish and insects as well as fossilised trees, plants and flowers. After about half a mile we were at the end of this disturbed area and found a path leading back up the banking.

Two rainy weeks later, we returned to look at the rocks, only to find that the river was in spate. The roar from the angry raging Liddel told us that our previous route would be not just inadvisable but impossible! Indeed, the rushing roaring waters had filled the bed of the Liddel, while spray was being flung up 30 feet to our precarious stance.

But all was not lost. We could still continue our walk along the excellent new paths above the Liddel for half a mile to a fork, where we chose the right-hand route leading away from the river. The path became a track and the track became a road which led down to Crookholm. However, we turned right towards the Copshaw road, which we joined near Archerbeck.

We turned right for half a mile past Harelawhole and right again for another half-mile back to Penton Bridge and the end of an enjoyable outing.

Deep winter at Carewoodrig

22: TANSY HILL AND ARRESGILL

This walk can be either six or ten miles long and consists of hill ground and track.

Three miles along the Lockerbie road we carefully parked the car at Wauchope Schoolhouse, although we could have taken it much further. As the name suggests, this had indeed been a school, but with the improvement in transport it closed more than half a century ago. For a short time the house had been called 'Seldom Inn' by some wit, but with a new occupant, it soon reverted to its original name. The Logan Water is an interesting little hill burn with a wealth of wildlife.

Near Cleuchfoot Cottages we crossed over the original Langholm to Galloway road, but had to look closely for what remained of the track. Immediately through the farm we departed from the river and turned right on to a track leading uphill along the Short Cleuch, continuing onwards at 20 degrees to Tansy Hill, where I have often looked for the plant of that name, but without success. From a distance, wild tansy looks remarkably like its relative, ragwort, for which it can easily be mistaken.

Looking across towards Cleuchfoot

Our next stop was on Fingland Knowe. In front of us lay the edge of a thick wood where the ubiquitous spruce trees went on for five miles before joining up with the much larger Castle O'er and Eskdalemuir Forests. However, at the Fingland Burn we walked downhill until we were back down to the Logan Water, which we had to cross near Arresgill. At this point we turned left along the road and so back to the Wauchope, after a six-mile walk.

By turning right we could have added a further four miles to our journey. Over the past forty years I have watched this forest grow and expand from seedlings to high marketable timber with the consequent but unfortunate loss of panoramas. Just past Arresgill we entered the forest and were confronted by three forest tracks. We chose the right-hand one and followed the winding and undulating road along the steep tree-clad hillside for two miles to where a road branched off downhill to the left. The old deserted cottage of Loganheid slowly and reluctantly came into sight deep in its hollow. The cottage is a sad sight as it crumbles and rots into oblivion, a victim of progress in communications. It is not so long since a family called Maxwell was born and raised here, and walked four miles to school each day. And thought nothing of it!

We turned down a faint path along the side of the burn. It was spring and wildlife was abundant with buzzard, bullfinch, cuckoo, peewit, oystercatcher, whaup and snipe. Blackcap, goldcrest, house martin, sand martin, sand piper and wheatear are resident all summer. This wee valley is locally noted for the profusion of mimulus, gowans, marsh marigolds, heartsease and primroses. Altogether a much favoured place.

Through this narrow glen where the heather and spruce-clad hills and shanks dropped steeply to the burn with eroded gullies tumbling betwixt them, traces of the old track began to reappear as it crossed and recrossed the meandering burn. But suddenly we turned a bend and we had returned to Arresgill with only an easy walk back to the car.

23: HARTSGARTH AND ROAN FELL

This walk is about 15 miles in length, 11 of which are on hill ground. But we needed an obliging 'Mrs Wanderer' to transport us to Hartsgarth Farm (OS79 494926) at the start of the walk. We drove through Newcastleton to The Smiddy Brig and Leahaugh Bridge, four miles up the Hermitage road, where Hartsgarth Farm is signposted to the left. After a word with George White, who kept us right about livestock, we passed through the farm, crossed to the northern side of the Hartsgarth Burn and headed west to the ruined Hazelyside Cottage.

Between the burn and the cottage were two water-filled depressions lined with rushes, an ideal spot for nesting ducks and waders. These ponds were created when a German bomber returning from a raid on Clydebank in 1941 released its remaining bomb load, possibly on seeing a careless light. Half a mile later we had crossed to the upper Hartsgarth Burn, where we reached higher and drier ground.

The intriguing thing about this small hollow in the shadow of the hills is the number of signs of ancient habitation and usage. The really old ones are in the form of earthworks with no apparent meaning or evident history. There are stells and dikes all around, some just a pile of stones and others in a good state of repair, while a few of them have small stone huts built on. We went across to some of the nearer ones. The huts are each about

A herd of wild goats

15 feet by about 10 feet and dyked in the same fashion as the stell itself, while the side walls are only about four feet high with a small square opening above the door to serve as a window. Two such stells are close together, one of which is reputed to have housed an illicit whisky still, but not even the smell remained.

We went on up the hillside where we saw many flat slabs on some of which were inscriptions such as biblical texts or the farmer's name; not just amateur scratchings as with a harrow tooth, but well designed and hewn. The stone huts had obviously been summer sheilings and perhaps one of the shepherds had at one time been a stonemason. There is also the cracked remnant of a huge grindstone which had been made in situ and had probably broken when rolled downhill.

The broken grindstone at Hartsgarth

From there we continued due west into a small corrie called the Trough Sike which 400 years ago was probably a 'beef tub', where stolen cattle could be hidden by the Reivers. Its other claim to fame is one of the many Peden's Stones from which Alexander 'Preacher' Peden is reputed to have addressed the local Covenanters in the 17th century. Among the rocks of this steep hillside we saw a few wild or feral goats and their kids. At Peden's Stone we took a bearing of 300 degrees onto the top of Roan Fell, where near the top there was a herd of around 16 feral goats. Being spring, we heard the lonely calls of whaups and golden plovers. From there we looked down into the Tarras Valley and further west into Eskdale while behind us lay Liddesdale with the Lake District and the Solway to the south.

Like many Border Hills, these tops are wet and can even be boggy with minute lochans stagnating among the peat and moss. But we headed due south to dry Millstone Edge, keeping to the east side of the boundary dyke or fence, and then went on south-west to Watch Hill and the Cooms Fell cairn, where we sheltered from the east wind while eating our bread and cheese. Our journey continued south-west through the rocky outcrops and a strong smell of goat, eventually reaching Tarras Lodge and the road to Langholm. While crossing the Middlemoss, a pair of low-level hunting hen harriers kept us distant company for part of the way. For the first mile Whita was in front but we soon left it behind as we headed past the MacDiarmid Memorial and back down into Langholm.

24: PEDEN'S VIEW

This is a fairly easy six-mile walk which should take about two and a half hours, but it will need boots or other strong footwear.

We followed a familiar route out of town along Thomas Telford Road, turning left past the Academy into Eskdaill Street and opposite the telephone box, we turned right up Jamie's Brae to Scott's Knowe. Corrie and I continued on up the hill until we reached a gate leading onto Meikleholm Hill. At this point I was able to look over the nearby trees and see right down Eskdale almost to the Solway, and as we climbed higher, the panorama grew wider until the Solway, the northern Lake District and even the Galloway Hills slowly swam into view. In late summer, the flowers seemed to have flitted from the low meadows and holms onto the alpine meadows and hillsides. Meikleholm is an exceptional spot for wild orchids, with hundreds of spotted and purple varieties on the southern slopes.

Just below the water tank we followed the track round to the right until I could see a small cairn about 200 yards due north. By now the winding track was deteriorating until we left it to pass the cairn on our right. A different aspect of the Eskdale hills was

Langholm from Peden's View

appearing with Ettrick Pen, Tudhope Hill and Crumpton away on the skyline, while nearer at hand we had Timpen and Potholm Hill. Just past the wee cairn the trod started to drop through the hawthorn and rowan trees until we reached the small March Burn (a march, incidentally, is a boundary).

The March Burn is a bit glaury, and once over this obstacle it is a short but steep climb out of the cleuch. As you climb, the scenery along the Esk opens out to Potholm with Barntalloch sitting at the bottom of Bauchle Hill. For those who like something for nothing in the form of wild raspberries and brambles, this half-mile track down to the road is a delicious paradise each autumn. Below us on the Castle Holms were about 25 commercial breeding and rearing pens for pheasants.

We reached the Eskdalemuir road and turned left to walk up the slope for about half a mile. Just after the Craigcleuch Quarry, we went through the gate on the right and so onto the hillside. It was quite a stiff climb up the wee hill on our right, but it wasn't very long before we stood on Peden's View where yet another panorama presented itself.

Alexander Peden was a minister in Galloway during the Covenanting times in the mid 17th century who refused to read from the English Book of Common Prayer. In consequence, he was banished from his church and became an itinerant preacher, always on the run from the authorities, preaching at 'conventicles' as they were known. These assemblies took place in hidden glens and on hillsides such as this one, and there are several Peden's Views and Peden's Stones marked on OS maps of Southern Scotland. It is said that while the troops searched the valleys and hills, Peden sat and watched them from Peden's View. This of course cannot be correct, as the viewpoint is lower than all the surrounding hilltops.

Peden was nicknamed 'The Prophet' but in 1673 his luck ran out and he was captured. He was imprisoned on the Bass Rock for four years, then put on a ship bound for America. However, he managed to leave the ship in London and made his way back to Scotland to resume his fugitive existence. He died in 1686 aged about 60 and the dragoons suspended his body from a gibbet on Cumnock Hill in Ayrshire. The spot became known as the Hill of Reproach.

Reflecting on those turbulent times, we made our way to the top of Clark Fell where, after looking at traces of a larach, we headed downhill and due north into the corner of the Cushat Wood. We could find no evidence of cushiedoos. On previous visits I had seen the odd cushie, but not on this occasion. Readers may be wondering 'What on earth is a cushie? I've never heard of a cushat, let alone a cushiedoo'. These are all local names for the large wild wood pigeon.

We walked through the Cushat Wood where the sole inhabitants appeared to be pheasants. Almost immediately through the second gate lay another and much bigger

The bright white flower of Ramsons, or Wild Garlic

larach of an ancient settlement (OS79 253873). It was pear-shaped, about 150 feet by 120 feet, and contained evidence of some ancient buildings, though whether they were built 400 or 4,000 years ago I had no means of knowing.

A hundred yards below this larach and just across from Milnholm Farm, a gate gave access to the public road. We turned right and in a mile joined the main road. Near this point a sign indicated a route through the wall and along an old path, long disused but now being restored, down to the Esk at the Duchess Bridge and so back to Langholm.

25: TARRAS WATER AND WHITA

This is a walk of about nine miles, but it is all on good paths, tracks or roads. From the Kilngreen we passed the Town Hall and followed the main road south until, past Ashley Bank House we bore left up the Hall Path, but at the next two forks kept straight on to a track parallel to the old railway line. We passed the 'Roon Hoose' which was at one time an old stone summerhouse, then walked through a wood of natural sessile oaks. Once through the farm of Broomholmshiels, we turned left and followed the road uphill until we could look down into the Lower Tarras Valley. This has been designated a Site of Special Scientific Interest where you might see green woodpeckers, short-eared owls, tawny owls, buzzards, hawks and flycatchers.

As we walked on down the hill road to the river, we kept an eye open for foxes, deer or mink. We crossed the Rashiel Bridge, and noticed the river terraces where the river has changed course over the millennia. Near the top of the hill, the road crossed an old man-made channel. This is the beginning of the Tarras Aqueduct, as described in chapter 3.

By now we were back into cultivated fields for a short time and passed through the farm of Cronksbank, where the going underfoot changed from tarmac to a stony track. As a

The tumbling Tarras Water

cronk is an old name for a jenny heron, we looked around for some, but there were none in evidence. Just across the Tarras two isolated but conjoined fields broke up the hillside. They looked rather like an open book, as did another nearby field; indeed, they are known locally as 'The Bibles'.

The track led us easily on to Perterburn, where we turned left through a gate and walked down to a smaller gate and a footbridge across the Tarras leading to Middlemoss. Just upriver from here is a ford which can be used when the water is low, but the footbridge is always there in case the river is high. From Middlemoss it is a straightforward walk along the track above the Tarras, as described in

The beautiful Bellfower, or Campanula

chapter 16. As we walked over the Tarras Muir, much evidence of peat cutting could be seen, some of very recent origin. In just over half a mile our track joined the hill road to Copshaw; we turned left, heading back towards the Muckle Toon.

One benefit of a smooth road is that we were able to look around yet still keep walking. The muir is a favoured spot for many birds. As we walked I saw a large bird flying low over the heather, in and out of the small sikes and over the knowes. It was a male hen harrier with its silver-grey plumage and pure white rump. Away up the glen a short-eared owl was tumbling and diving in a late mating display, while a whaup called its mournful lay.

The White Yett at the summit of the road looked far away, but we were soon enough there. I had a quick look at Hugh MacDiarmid's Memorial and tried to associate the shapes with his poems; but Corrie was just not interested. It was all downhill from then on until we reached the trees. Just past an old, overgrown quarry beside the road we turned left onto a path which leads past a sheep stell to the top of the Whita Road and the golf course.

Before long, we were down the hill and back to the Market Place in Langholm.

26: TINNIS HILL AND THE HORNED CAIRN

This walk is mainly moorland and road and is about 15 miles long, but could be shortened to nine miles by arranging a lift to Tinnis Bridge, halfway to Newcastleton, which town is sometimes referred to as Copshawholm.

From Langholm's Kilngreen we walked half a mile to Milntown from where we followed the Newcastleton road past the MacDiarmid Memorial. This is in the form of a huge open book where we tried to understand the symbolic references to aspects of Hugh MacDiarmid and his writings. Just over the cattle grid we were lucky to see a couple of hen harriers quartering the hillside and a little later, higher in the sky, we watched a short-eared owl as it displayed, rolling and tumbling.

The road stretched out before us for another four miles with views of the Debateable Lands along the Border. We walked past Little Tarras and the peat diggings until we reached the Tarras in the depth of its little glen. This is one of my favourite places for wildlife such as owls, buzzards, harriers, grouse, golden plovers, chats, pipits and larks. I always keep a wary eye open for adders and mink, too.

Looking towards Tinnis Hill

Down we went to Tarras Lodge on its hairpin bend and back up to Tinnis Bridge with Tinnis Hill standing sentinel, to the south. After the hard road we were relieved to take to the heather muir, in season a mass of bog-cotton, bog asphodel or orchids. But the walking was no easier with patches of sphagnum moss and reeds between the burns. It was a case of down and up, down and up. But in half a mile we were onto the slopes of lonely Tinnis Hill. From the top we had a fine view right up and down Liddesdale from Maiden Pap to Kershopefoot.

From Tinnis Hill we walked another half mile due south to a corner of Tinnisburn Forest (OS79 431845) where we followed the edge for a short distance south to another corner and entered the spruce trees. After a short, rough walk through the trees we reached a forest road along Windy Edge. There are three stone artifacts in this area. The trees had grown since my last visit but almost straight in front we made out a large canted stone perhaps ten feet tall. This Boundary Stane is the northern limit of the Debateable Lands between England and Scotland, dating from the time of the Reivers.

We calculated that the ancient Long Cairn or Horned Cairn should lie about 500 yards to the west. Right enough, there appeared to be a grassy track through the spruce trees, and indeed it led us right to a pile of rounded stones. This cairn was about one hundred feet in length by about fifteen feet broad. Then we noticed that it had in fact some semblance of shape with two rounded parts at one end akin to horns. It is nowhere near as well preserved as those on Orkney, yet on this windy, lonely muirland it was quite eerie. It can be approached more easily from Underburnmouth and Whisgills to the south of Copshaw.

According to the map a 'Monument' lies at a bearing of 110 degrees from the cairn. We eventually found it half a mile away among the briars and brambles and spruces and ditches, but it was only about two feet tall. The inscription states that one Michael Dixon known as 'Sclater' had been walking from Whisgills to Millsteads to a wedding on the 29th July 1805 when a thunderstorm blew up on the bare Windy Ridge and he was killed by lightning. The word 'Sclater' could be a nickname as it is Scots for a woodlouse!

From there we returned to the edge of the wood and followed it west for about a mile until we came to the source of the Raegill Burn. This eventually led us to the Tarras just downstream from the Rashiel Brig. Upstream from the bridge at the cattle grid we followed the cleuch and then the dyke uphill to the west, past St Ringan's Well (the patron Saint of lost causes) until on top of the slope we went through the gate and on to the top of Whita. From there it was down the path to Whita Well and the Kirk Wynd where we had started.

27: LANGHOLM TO MEIKLEDALE

This walk consists of three easy miles on a woodland track and 11 miles on heather hills. Corrie and I followed a familiar route through Langfauld Woods as far as Potholm farmhouse where we turned sharp right back uphill to our original track, having bypassed a collapsed stone bridge. While near the farm we called in at Staplegordon Churchyard to look for its escape hole in the wall to be used on the Day of Judgment. The hole had been designed by a disabled man who was worried that when the Great Call came, he might be left behind when the others "louped ower the wa's". Unfortunately for his sake the hole has been infilled to keep out the sheep. The remains of Barntalloch Castle are also worth a visit.

Half a mile later we crossed the Sorbie Hass road and headed up the west side of the Mill Burn to its source on Bauchle Hill (meaning Herdsman's Hill) where there was an entrancing view of the Solway, the English Lakes and the Border Hills. This is a popular spot to see buzzards or kestrels, or even the occasional golden eagle. After a gradual climb we reached a fence and followed it down into the bealach or saddle, where a small gate at the corner of a wood gave access to Sorbie Hope.

Mist over Eskdale

From the gate we continued alongside the spruce trees, eventually reaching the top of Crumpton Hill where I recall with some embarrassment my telling a group of walkers from Hawick to "mind the bog!" - and promptly fell in. So be warned! From Crumpton the route followed the fence as it undulated roughly along the 1500 foot height; much of it was rough heather and much of the fence appeared to be electrified. We plodded on northwards down Meg's Shank to Longgrain Head. A quarter of a mile north from here a headstone commemorates the feat of a silly woman called Lady Florance Custs who rode her horse down the very steep slope. We took a heading of 320 degrees to Mellion Muir and then north to Wolfhopehead, from where we could see down Stennieswater and up Eskdalemuir to Ettrick Pen.

The fence guided us onwards to Broadhead and Middlehill with the forestry road from Bush o' Ewes to Stennieswater crossing in between. We continued in a north-easterly direction to Blackgrain and Swingle Height, which is a corruption of Swine Gill. At Rashiegrain we reached the Roxburgh border, with only half a mile to Pikethaw, where we looked down into the bealach of Ewes Doors between the Eweslees Burn and the Wrangway Burn. It is an intriguing place with ancient remains from over a long period of time.

The surrounding hills are of typical Borders shape with steep, scarred, tiring slopes and rounded tops while the cleuchs and shanks have names like Merry Path, Haggis Side and Maiden Paps. Ewes Doors itself is reputed to be the site of a hermitage belonging to the Over Church of Ewes down in the valley at Unthank. As it was early spring and the bracken was still a bronze carpet with thrusting new spears of green, we were able to look down on a prehistoric burial tumulus as well as 250 yards of lineal earthworks.

From Pikethaw we walked south-east along the hilltops to Frodaw and then south down to Meikledale Farm. It was still a fine clear day; clear enough to appreciate the views of Arkleton Craigs on the other side of the Esk. Where the march dike reached Bankend Wood, a hard walker would have turned left down to Mosspeeble and continued south over the opposite hills, but on the last occasion I chickened out and caught a bus from Meikledale Haugh, back to Langholm. We returned next day to complete our walk down the east side of Ewesdale as described in chapter 28. There are several B&Bs in the upper valley where a walker could spend a comfortable night.

28: MEIKLEDALE TO LANGHOLM

This is a walk of ten miles, three of which are on good roads, the remainder being on heather covered high muirland. The walk in chapter 27 had ended at Meikledale Farm road end (OS79 378926), which is where we took it up once more. We walked up the A7 road for over a quarter of a mile and took the farm road down to Mosspeeble. The road round the farm buildings is obvious so we followed it across the burn and up to the cottage where we had a look at the large circular earthworks which almost surround the building. Shortly afterwards the road divided, and we continued up the right fork to the fence.

Our route climbed onwards for a mile along the south side of Baraman's Cleuch until it reached Rowantree Cove. About half a mile to the north, the most prominent feature is a deep gully known as Bloody Cleuch. According to legend, the dragoons slew a party of Reivers and so caused the burn to turn red with blood, as it still on occasion remains. It may be just a coincidence that the burn rises in a banking of deep red clay. From Rowantree Cove it was only a quarter of a mile at 160 degrees to the top of Arkleton Hill (OS79 405922). By this time we were walking along the edge of the 'Debateable Lands', the 16th century haunt and refuge of the Border Reivers. In those far-off days, the then wooded Tarras Valley had been an almost impregnable stronghold of these lawless families.

Our route continued along Arkleton Hill, passing Black Cove and Upper Nick before descending south to Auldshiels Wood, over Duncan Sike and up again to Hog Fell. From there it was a slow descent along the fence and the dyke and through the deep heather looking down on Glendivan, Hoghill and Terrona until we reached the road down to Langholm. From this belvedere the Ewes Valley and surrounding hills were arrayed in all their beauty. We ignored the tarmac road and followed the rough track from the MacDiarmid Memorial to the top of Whita and the Malcolm Memorial obelisk, simply known as 'The Monument', where we turned right and followed the path towards the Solway and steeply down into Langholm and the end of another splendid walk.

A rainbow arcs over Whita Hill

WALKING WITH WANDERER